Contents

Preface   2

Chapter One: The Art and Models of Effective Communication   5

Chapter Two: The Power of Word   19

Chapter Three: Language and Structure Essentials for Business Communication   32

Chapter Four: Fundamentals of Business Writing   42

Chapter Five: Persuasive Writing in Business   52

Chapter Six: Bridging Cultures: Mastering Cross-Cultural Communication   63

Chapter Seven: Crafting Impact: Writing for Digital and Social Media Success   74

Chapter Eight: Effective Communication Strategies for Crisis Management   85

Chapter Nine: Crisis Management Mastery: Techniques and Writing Skills for Success   94

Chapter Ten: Persuasive Presentations: Strategies for Meaningful Communication   103

References   119

Preface

Communication is the currency of leadership. It enables the translation of vision into action, the alignment of diverse stakeholders toward shared goals, and the resolution of conflicts with integrity and understanding. In today's interconnected world, where challenges and opportunities alike span continents and cultures, the ability to communicate effectively is not just a skill—it is an essential leadership trait. This book, *Communicate to Lead: Business English for the Next Generation*, is designed to equip aspiring leaders with the tools they need to navigate the complexities of modern business communication with confidence and purpose.

Throughout my career as a business communication expert, I have observed the evolving demands placed on leaders in the global business landscape. While technical expertise and strategic insight remain vital, it is often the ability to inspire, persuade, and connect through communication that defines exceptional leaders. Yet, many emerging professionals face a persistent challenge: how to communicate their ideas effectively in a professional setting, particularly when English is the medium of choice in global business.

This book addresses this challenge head-on, offering a practical and comprehensive guide to mastering business English for leadership. Drawing upon years of experience and interaction with professionals from diverse industries and backgrounds, *Communicate to Lead* distills the principles, strategies, and techniques that leaders need to thrive in environments where clarity, persuasion, and authenticity are paramount.

The chapters in this book are organized to address the full spectrum of communication scenarios that leaders encounter, from managing internal teams to engaging external stakeholders. We explore the nuances of crafting persuasive proposals, writing with impact in digital environments, handling crises with poise, and delivering presentations that resonate. These are not abstract discussions; they are practical lessons rooted in real-world examples and enriched by case studies, templates, and exercises that you can apply immediately to your professional journey.

One of the unique aspects of *Communicate to Lead* is its focus on the next generation of leaders. Today's business world is markedly different from that of a decade ago. Globalization, technological advancements, and heightened ethical expectations have reshaped the way organizations operate and communicate. Leaders must be adept at navigating these shifts, crafting messages that resonate across cultures, leveraging digital tools to connect with audiences, and addressing ethical considerations with transparency and responsibility. This book embraces these realities, preparing readers to lead in a dynamic, interconnected, and rapidly evolving environment.

But this is not merely a book about skills. It is a call to recognize the profound power of communication to shape relationships, influence change, and build trust. Whether you are delivering a presentation, responding to a crisis, or crafting a strategic email, your words carry weight. They reflect your values, your vision, and your credibility as a leader. This book will help you harness that power effectively, ensuring your communication aligns with your leadership goals.

As you engage with the content of this book, I encourage you to view it not as a checklist of techniques but as a foundation for continuous growth. Communication is an art as much as it is a skill, requiring constant refinement and adaptation. The insights provided here are designed to be adaptable, allowing you to tailor them to your unique style, audience, and challenges.

I am deeply grateful to the countless professionals, colleagues, and learners who have contributed to the development of the ideas and strategies presented in this book. Their questions, feedback, and experiences have enriched my understanding of effective communication and inspired me to write this book. It is my hope that *Communicate to Lead* will serve as a meaningful resource on your journey to becoming an exceptional communicator and leader.

In closing, I leave you with this thought: leadership is about more than making decisions or achieving goals. It is about building bridges—between people, ideas, and possibilities. Communication is the tool that allows us to construct those bridges. Through this book, I hope to empower you to communicate with clarity, authenticity, and impact, leading not just with words but with purpose.

Welcome to *Communicate to Lead: Business English for the Next Generation*—your companion in mastering the art of communication for the future of leadership.

Dr. Joseph W.C. Lau, Chartered Linguist, DBA, CMgr, FCIL
Author

Chapter One:

The Art and Models of Effective Communication

Effective communication stands as a cornerstone of both personal and professional success, fundamentally shaping how we interact, collaborate, and build relationships. It transcends the simple act of exchanging information; instead, it is a nuanced process that involves the articulation of ideas, feelings, and thoughts through various methods—verbal, non-verbal, written, and visual.

In a world that thrives on connection, the ability to communicate effectively can significantly impact outcomes in every aspect of life. Whether negotiating a business deal, leading a team, or fostering personal relationships, the precision and clarity of our words matter immensely. Equally crucial is ensuring that the intended message is not only transmitted but also received and understood accurately by others. This dynamic interplay is where effective communication shines—acting as the bridge that connects individuals and facilitates mutual understanding.

As we explore the importance of effective communication, we'll delve into its various dimensions, examining how clarity, active listening, emotional intelligence, and non-verbal cues play pivotal roles in fostering successful interactions. By understanding these elements, we can harness the power of communication to enhance collaboration, resolve conflicts, and inspire action in both personal and professional contexts. In doing so, we acknowledge that effective communication is not just an essential skill; it is a vital force driving relationships, innovation, and success in our interconnected world.

The Foundations of Communication

Communication takes multiple forms, each with its unique characteristics and applications:

- **Verbal Communication**: The spoken word, either in person or via technological mediums, forms the basis of verbal communication. It is essential for face-to-face discussions, phone calls, and presentations.

- **Written Communication**: From emails to reports, written communication conveys messages through text. Clarity, grammar, and style are crucial to ensure that the intended meaning is properly understood.

- **Non-Verbal Communication**: Body language, gestures, facial expressions, and even silence play an influential role in conveying messages. Non-verbal cues often provide more insight into emotions and intentions than words do.

- **Visual Communication**: The use of images, symbols, videos, and visual aids helps to communicate complex ideas efficiently. Visuals can evoke emotions and clarify intricate information.

Understanding these different types of communication allows us to choose the best method for each specific context, ensuring that our message reaches its intended audience effectively.

Business Communication: A Unique Dimension

In a business context, communication takes on additional significance. **Business communication** refers to the sharing of information between people within and outside a company to achieve specific organizational goals. Whether it is in the form of emails, reports, meetings, or presentations, effective business communication is pivotal to a company's success. It connects various stakeholders, aligns objectives, and facilitates decision-making processes.

Engaging Stakeholders

A key aspect of business communication involves understanding and addressing the needs of stakeholders. **Stakeholders** are individuals or groups with a vested interest in a company's activities, performance, and outcomes. They can be classified as:

- **Internal Stakeholders**: These are individuals within the organization, such as employees, managers, and shareholders. Their involvement in the company's operations gives them a direct stake in its performance.

- **External Stakeholders**: These include customers, suppliers, investors, regulators, and the broader community. While they are not directly involved in the company's operations, their interests are impacted by the company's actions.

By effectively communicating with both internal and external stakeholders, businesses can enhance trust, foster collaboration, and ultimately contribute to long-term sustainability and success.

People Within and Outside the Company

Within a company, individuals are generally referred to as **employees, team members**, or **personnel**. The specific role someone plays may vary depending on their position and responsibilities—e.g., **managers, executives**, or **workers**.

Outside the organization, individuals are recognized as **customers**, **clients**, **suppliers**, **vendors**, **investors**, or even just the **public**. Understanding these distinctions helps a company tailor its communications appropriately to different groups, ensuring that the messages resonate and lead to constructive outcomes.

The Importance of Business Communication Skills

Good business communication skills are invaluable. They:

- **Build trust and credibility** with clients and colleagues.

- **Facilitate teamwork and collaboration**, promoting a cohesive work environment.

- **Enhance professional image** and reputation, which is critical for career advancement.

- **Improve customer relationships and loyalty**, leading to a more successful business.

- **Boost productivity and efficiency** by reducing misunderstandings and enabling smooth workflow.

Style in Communication

Style in communication refers to how we present our message, including the formality, tone, and word choice used to suit a specific audience or purpose:

- **Formality**: This involves deciding on the level of formality depending on the context. Formal situations may require sophisticated vocabulary and structured language, whereas informal settings may benefit from more casual and approachable wording.

- **Tone and Voice**: The tone reflects the emotional quality of your communication, while voice represents the distinct style that characterizes how you express yourself.

- **Word Choice**: Specific word choices and sentence structure impact how your message is perceived and can help in achieving the desired effect, whether informative, persuasive, or expressive.

Formal vs. Informal Styles

Formal and informal styles of communication are distinguished by their structure, vocabulary, and intended audience, each suited to specific contexts. The formal style adheres to conventions of syntax and grammar, using precise language and a systematic structure that emphasizes clarity and professionalism. This style is typically utilized in academic writing, legal documents, and professional correspondence, where the objective is to convey information or analysis in a serious and objective manner.

Conversely, informal style is characterized by a more relaxed tone, incorporating conversational language, colloquialisms, and a less rigid sentence structure. This style is often employed in personal communications, such as text messages, casual emails, and social media interactions, where the emphasis lies on relatability and ease of expression. The choice between these styles is crucial, as it significantly impacts the effectiveness of communication and how the message is received by the audience. Understanding the nuances of each style allows for appropriate tailoring of discourse to suit various contexts and audiences.

- **Formal Style**: Often used in official reports, business proposals, and communications with authority figures. It avoids contractions, uses sophisticated language, and aims for professionalism.

- **Informal Professional Style**: Typically used in emails, instant messaging, or casual meetings. It emphasizes clarity and directness, using plain English to ensure better understanding and foster approachability.

Context, Purpose, and Audience

Effective communication requires understanding the **context** in which it occurs, the **purpose** behind it, and the **audience** receiving the message.

- **Context**: Refers to the situation and background where the communication takes place.

- **Purpose**: Represents the reason for communicating, such as to inform, persuade, or resolve an issue.

- **Audience**: Understanding the audience's needs, expectations, and characteristics is crucial for delivering effective communication.

Reflecting on Your Communication Style

To improve your communication skills, reflect on your own style. Consider questions such as:

- What are your strengths and weaknesses in communication?

- How do you adapt your communication style when interacting with different audiences?

- Are there any areas where you feel you need improvement?

- Can you recall a situation where effective communication helped resolve a conflict? What strategies did you use?

Types of Communication: Accidental, Expressive, and Rhetorical

1. **Accidental Communication**: Occurs without intention. For instance, unintended eye contact between a boss and an employee might convey unspoken messages. Non-verbal cues often fall into this category.

2. **Expressive Communication**: Used to express emotions rather than exchange ideas. An employee exclaiming, "*Thank God it's Friday!*" communicates excitement but is not meant to exchange information.

3. **Rhetorical Communication**: Involves deliberate attempts to influence or persuade, such as an employee negotiating a raise. This type of communication is often used strategically in business.

The Rhetorical Model of Communication

The **rhetorical model** involves the following components:

1. **Sender**: The source of the message.

2. **Objective**: The purpose for communicating.

3. **Receiver**: The target audience.

4. **Message**: The information being conveyed.

5. **Interpreted Message**: How the audience understands the message.

6. **Channel**: The medium used for communication.

7. **Feedback**: The response from the receiver.

8. **Environment/Context**: The physical and social setting.

9. **Noise**: Anything that disrupts effective communication.

Prominent Models of Communication in Business

To fully understand communication's role in business and personal interactions, we need to delve into various communication models and frameworks that provide insight into how messages are conveyed, received, and interpreted. These models serve as a foundation for understanding the complexity and dynamics of effective communication, highlighting the need for adaptability and awareness of the factors that can enhance or hinder successful exchanges.

The Linear Model of Communication

The **Linear Model of Communication** is one of the simplest frameworks, depicting communication as a one-way process where information flows from sender to receiver. This model has been fundamental in shaping our understanding of communication, and its key components include:

- **Sender**: The originator of the message, who encodes and transmits information.

- **Message**: The content that is being communicated, whether it be information, ideas, or emotions.

- **Channel**: The medium used to deliver the message, such as spoken words, written text, or visual media.

- **Receiver**: The individual or audience intended to receive the message.

- **Noise**: Any factor that can distort or hinder the transmission and interpretation of the message, such as environmental distractions or misunderstanding.

The **Shannon-Weaver Model** is an example of a linear communication model. Developed in 1948, this model emphasizes the technical aspects of communication, such as encoding, transmission, and decoding (Shannon & Weaver, 1949). Although this model laid the groundwork for communication theory, it does not account for feedback or the interactive nature of real-world communication, making it a more limited representation of complex human exchanges.

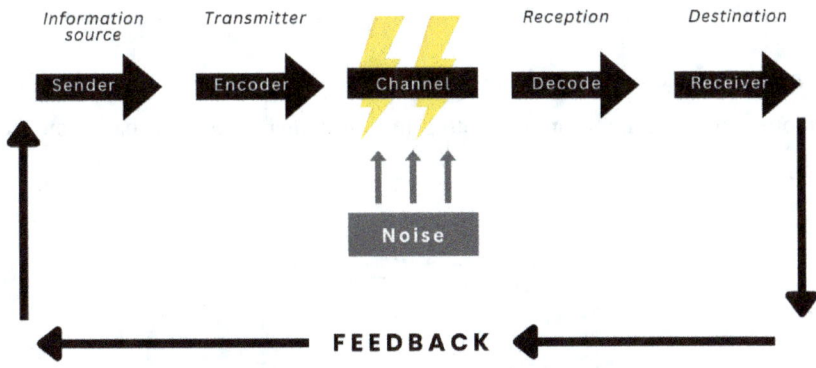

SHANNON-WEAVER'S MODEL OF COMMUNICATION

Interactive and Transactional Models of Communication

While the linear model provided a foundation, **interactive** and **transactional models** expanded upon this by recognizing the importance of feedback and the dynamic relationship between the sender and receiver. These models emphasize the continuous flow of communication, the shared roles of the sender and receiver, and the impact of context on how messages are conveyed and understood.

Schramm's Interactive Model

Wilbur Schramm's Model of Communication emphasizes the exchange of messages between communicators and introduces the concept of **feedback** (Schramm, 1954). Schramm's model highlights the following components:

- **Encoders and Decoders**: In Schramm's view, both communicators encode and decode messages, and communication occurs when there is a shared understanding or common experience between them.

- **Field of Experience**: This concept reflects the background, experiences, culture, and perceptions of each communicator. Effective communication requires a degree of overlap between the fields of experience of the sender and receiver, allowing for a common understanding of the message.

- **Feedback**: The addition of feedback to the communication process allows for a two-way flow of information, enabling communicators to adjust their messages based on the receiver's response.

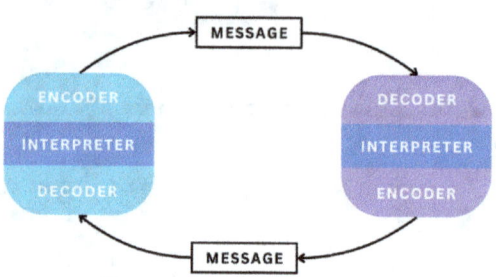

The interactive model acknowledges that communication is not just about sending and receiving messages but also about adjusting and adapting based on the audience's reactions.

Berlo's SMCR Model (1960)

The **Berlo SMCR Model** (Source, Message, Channel, Receiver) provides a more detailed understanding of how communication occurs by focusing on:

- **Source**: The individual or group originating the message. Effective communication depends on the source's skills, attitudes, and knowledge.

- **Message**: The content and form of the information being conveyed. This includes the message's structure, elements, content, and treatment.

- **Channel**: The medium used to convey the message, such as verbal, written, or visual means. Sensory channels (e.g., hearing, sight) play a significant role in how messages are interpreted.

- **Receiver**: The target audience, whose understanding and interpretation of the message are influenced by their attitudes, skills, and knowledge.

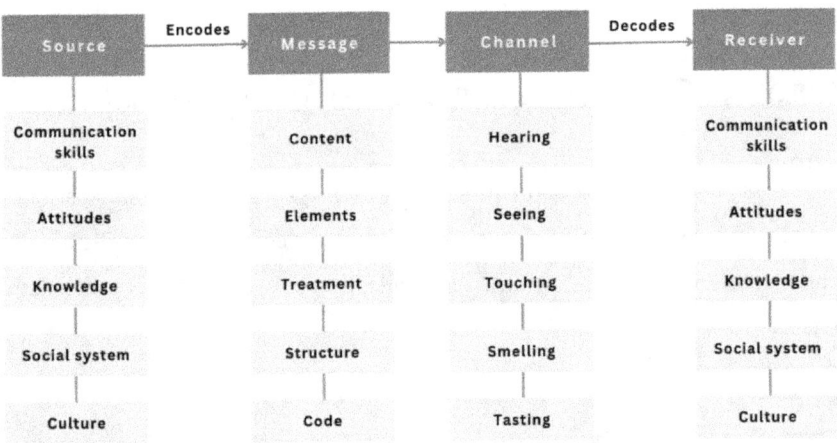

The SMCR model emphasizes that communication success is dependent on alignment between the sender's and receiver's fields of experience, as well as their ability to encode and decode messages   accurately.

Transactional Model of Communication

The **Transactional Model** goes a step further by viewing communication as a simultaneous, continuous process where all participants are both senders and receivers. Communication here is not linear but rather a **transaction** in which participants create meaning through constant feedback loops. Key features of the transactional model include:

- **Simultaneous Roles**: Communicators play the roles of sender and receiver concurrently, continuously influencing each other.

- **Environment and Context**: This model places significant emphasis on context—both the physical and social environments in which communication occurs. The relationship between communicators affects how messages are understood.

- **Noise and Barriers**: Like earlier models, the transactional model acknowledges the impact of noise. However, it also considers the barriers arising from social, cultural, and psychological factors that can affect the interpretation of messages.

Rhetorical Communication and Persuasion Models

In business contexts, **rhetorical communication** plays a significant role, particularly when attempting to persuade or influence stakeholders. Understanding the rhetorical model of communication helps in crafting messages that are not only informative but also impactful and convincing.

Aristotle's Model of Persuasion

Aristotle, the ancient Greek philosopher, developed a model of communication focused on rhetoric—the art of persuasion (Aristotle, trans. Freese, 1926). His model emphasizes three key elements:

- **Ethos**: The credibility and trustworthiness of the speaker.

- **Pathos**: The emotional appeal used to connect with the audience.

- **Logos**: The logical structure and argument presented in the message.

In the business world, using **ethos** can build trust with stakeholders, **pathos** can create emotional resonance with customers, and **logos** can demonstrate the reasoning behind strategic decisions. Successful business communicators often use a combination of these elements to achieve their goals.

The Role of Feedback in Communication Models

Feedback is a critical element in ensuring the effectiveness of communication. Whether it is verbal or non-verbal, immediate or delayed, feedback provides the sender with insights into how the message was received and understood.

In an organizational setting, **upward feedback** from employees to management helps in identifying challenges and improving processes, while **downward feedback** from management ensures that employees are informed and guided towards organizational objectives. Effective feedback is constructive, specific, and timely, contributing to better understanding and continuous improvement in communication practices.

Applying Communication Models in Business Scenarios

To better understand how these communication models can be applied, consider the following scenarios:

1. **Internal Team Meeting**: During a project meeting, the **transactional model** comes into play as team members continuously exchange ideas, provide feedback, and make decisions. The success of the meeting depends on the team leader's ability to facilitate two-way communication, address misunderstandings (noise), and ensure that everyone is aligned.

2. **Sales Presentation**: A sales manager giving a presentation to potential clients might use **Aristotle's model of persuasion** to craft an effective pitch—establishing credibility (ethos), connecting emotionally with the audience (pathos), and providing solid evidence for the product's benefits (logos).

3. **Crisis Communication**: During a crisis, clear communication is critical. The **linear model** may be employed to deliver urgent messages to the public. However, feedback mechanisms, such as social media responses, allow for more interactive communication to address concerns and adjust the approach as necessary.

Key Takeaways from Communication Models

Understanding various communication models helps communicators identify the strengths and weaknesses of their approach, adapt their strategies for different contexts, and ensure that messages are effectively conveyed and understood. By incorporating **feedback**, **context**, and **receiver expectations**, business professionals can enhance their communication skills and make interactions more meaningful and successful.

Chapter Two:

The Power of Word

In the fast-paced world of business, effective communication serves as the bedrock for successful interactions and relationships. The words we choose to convey our messages carry a unique power that can influence perceptions, drive decisions, and foster collaboration. Whether it's a persuasive sales pitch, a clear email, or a crucial presentation, the right words can inspire confidence, create engagement, and motivate teams to achieve collective goals. Conversely, poorly chosen words can lead to misunderstandings, damaged relationships, and lost opportunities.

In this exploration of the power of words in business communication, we will examine how language shapes company culture, affects negotiation outcomes, and influences brand perception. We will delve into various aspects of communication—verbal and written—highlighting the importance of tone, clarity, and emotional intelligence in crafting meaningful messages. For instance, the way leaders articulate a vision can galvanize employees and stakeholders alike, while the language used in marketing campaigns can authenticate a brand's voice and build loyalty among customers.

Furthermore, we will discuss the growing importance of digital communication in today's business environment, where emails, social media, and virtual meetings have become the norm. The efficiency of these platforms demands that professionals be even more deliberate about their word choices, as misinterpretations can easily occur without non-verbal cues. Through case studies and real-world examples, we will illustrate how effective business communication can lead to innovative solutions and successful outcomes, and how the power of words—carefully crafted and thoughtfully delivered—can create a lasting impact in the corporate landscape

As we navigate through this discussion, it becomes evident that mastering the art of business communication is not only about conveying information; it is about harnessing the power of words to inspire action, build trust, and drive success in an increasingly interconnected world.

Definition of Word Power:

- **Key Concept**: Word power refers to a person's vocabulary and ability to choose appropriate words for effective communication. It is not merely about having an extensive vocabulary, but also about knowing when and how to use the right words to convey the intended message.
- **Importance**: In the workplace, word power reflects a manager's professionalism, confidence, and leadership potential. The ability to use precise language ensures clarity, reduces misunderstandings, and inspires confidence in others.
- **Context**: This chapter will explore how vocabulary and grammar influence business communication, how they impact the perception of professionalism, and the techniques to enhance one's word power for improved communication in business settings.

The Importance of Vocabulary in the Workplace

Enhancing Clarity in Communication:

Effective communication starts with clarity, and vocabulary plays a pivotal role in ensuring that the message is clear and easily understood. The ability to use precise vocabulary helps eliminate misunderstandings and reduces the chances of ambiguity.

- For example, instead of using generic terms like *"move forward,"* using more specific words like *"implement"* or *"execute"* clearly conveys the action to be taken.
- A manager who can clearly articulate goals, instructions, or feedback is more likely to foster a productive work environment where team members understand expectations and deliverables.

Aiding in Persuasion and Negotiation:

The right choice of words can significantly influence others' decisions. Business negotiations and persuasive communication rely heavily on the use of impactful vocabulary that resonates with the audience.

- For instance, during negotiations, using terms like *"mutually beneficial"* can help create a sense of collaboration and partnership, fostering a positive outcome.
- Words that evoke positive emotions, such as *"opportunity,"* *"growth,"* and *"success,"* can motivate stakeholders and employees to support ideas and initiatives.

Conveying Professionalism and Expertise:

A strong vocabulary positions a manager as knowledgeable and trustworthy. It also helps to establish authority and build credibility, especially when addressing stakeholders, clients, or colleagues.

- For example, using industry-specific terminology accurately demonstrates expertise and familiarity with the field, which can boost trust and confidence in a manager's abilities.
- Conversely, the use of vague or incorrect terminology can lead to doubts about one's competence, potentially undermining professional relationships.

Building Your Word Power

Techniques for Vocabulary Expansion:

Building vocabulary is an ongoing process that requires consistent effort and a deliberate approach. There are several effective techniques to enhance one's word power:

- **Reading Widely**: Engaging with a diverse range of business journals, literature, articles, and industry reports is one of the most effective ways to enhance vocabulary.
  - **Tip**: While reading, take note of unfamiliar words, look up their meanings, and practice using them in conversations or writing.

- o Reading not only exposes you to new words but also demonstrates how these words are used in context, helping you understand their nuances and appropriate usage.

- **Utilizing Vocabulary-Building Apps**: Apps like Quizlet or Anki offer a practical way to practice vocabulary daily. These tools allow you to create flashcards and quizzes that reinforce learning through repetition.
- o Consistent use of such apps can lead to steady vocabulary improvement, which can be particularly useful for business professionals aiming to enhance their communication skills.

- **Engaging in Discussions and Networking**: Actively participating in discussions, forums, or professional networking groups is another effective way to improve vocabulary.
- o Engaging in conversations with peers, mentors, and industry professionals provides an opportunity to use new words, refine understanding, and receive feedback on language use.

Creating a Personal Word Journal:

Maintaining a personal word journal is an excellent way to track vocabulary growth. In this journal, list new words, their meanings, and example sentences. Revisiting and revising this journal regularly can help reinforce retention and ensure that the words become a part of your active   vocabulary.

Common Vocabulary Pitfalls

Overuse of Jargon:

Jargon refers to specialized terminology used within a particular industry or profession. While jargon can be useful for communicating with peers who understand it, overuse can lead to confusion, especially when communicating with a broader audience.

- **Example**: Instead of using jargon like *"synergy,"* which may sound vague, use more straightforward terms like *"collaboration"* or *"teamwork"* when addressing a general audience.
- **Impact**: Excessive use of jargon can make communication seem exclusionary and can alienate stakeholders who are not familiar with specific terms. Clear and simple language ensures inclusivity and better comprehension.

Misunderstanding of Terms:

Some terms have multiple meanings depending on the context, and misunderstanding these meanings can lead to miscommunication.

- **Example**: The term *"leverage"* can mean using borrowed capital in finance, while in negotiation, it refers to having an advantageous position. Understanding the context is crucial to ensure accurate use of such terms.
- Misusing words not only leads to confusion but can also damage credibility, especially in critical communications like proposals or reports.

Using Complex Words Unnecessarily:

Using unnecessarily complex words can hinder communication rather than enhance it. The goal of communication is to be understood, and simplicity often leads to better understanding.

- **Example**: Instead of using *"ameliorate,"* which is less commonly used, opt for *"improve,"* which is more accessible to a wider audience.
- In business settings, the emphasis should be on clarity, and using overly complex language can create barriers to understanding and slow down decision-making processes.

Real-Life Scenario – Word Power in Action

Scenario Description:

A manager is preparing for a quarterly performance review meeting with stakeholders, where they need to present the company's achievements and challenges.

Situation:

- The manager uses precise metrics and data, such as *"Our Q2 sales increased by 20% compared to Q1,"* instead of vague terms like *"We did well."*
- They also provide clear recommendations for improvement, using specific terminology that conveys authority and knowledge of the subject matter.

Outcome:

- The use of precise language enhances clarity, helping stakeholders understand the company's progress and challenges without ambiguity.

- The manager's choice of words demonstrates their control over the situation, leading to positive feedback and increased confidence from stakeholders in their leadership.

Grammar Basics for Business Communication

Importance of Grammar in Professional Writing:

Grammar forms the backbone of effective writing. In a professional setting, proper grammar reflects credibility, attention to detail, and competence. Poor grammar, on the other hand, can distract readers from the intended message and negatively impact the writer's image.

- **Example**: An email that contains grammatical errors, such as *"Your welcome to attend"* instead of *"You're welcome to attend,"* can shift the focus from the content to the mistake, resulting in a loss of professionalism.

Key Grammar Rules to Remember

Subject-Verb Agreement:

Ensuring that the subject and verb agree in number is fundamental to maintaining grammatical accuracy.

- **Example**: *"The team is winning"* (singular subject and singular verb) versus *"The teams are winning"* (plural subject and plural verb).
- Consistent subject-verb agreement helps maintain clarity and coherence in sentences.

Correct Use of Tenses:

Maintaining consistent tense throughout a narrative is crucial for avoiding confusion.

- **Example**: If you begin a report in the past tense (*"The project was successful"*), do not switch to the present tense (*"The results are impressive"*) without a valid reason.
- Inconsistent tense usage can make the writing disjointed and difficult to follow.

Use of Articles:

Articles such as *"a," "an,"* and *"the"* help specify whether you are talking about something general or specific.

- **Example**: *"I saw a dog"* (could be any dog) versus *"I saw the dog"* (referring to a specific dog).
- Proper use of articles provides clarity and prevents ambiguity in communication.

Punctuation Rules:

Punctuation marks like commas, periods, apostrophes, and colons are essential tools for structuring sentences and conveying meaning.

- **Example**: *"Let's eat, Grandma"* versus *"Let's eat Grandma"* illustrates how commas can drastically change the meaning of a sentence.
- Correct punctuation enhances readability and ensures that the intended meaning is conveyed accurately.

Real-Life Scenario – Importance of Grammar

Scenario Description:

A manager sends an important proposal via email to a potential client, aiming to secure a new business partnership.

Situation:

- The email contains grammar errors such as *"Your welcome to contact me anytime"* instead of the correct *"You're welcome to contact me anytime."*
- Additionally, the proposal includes run-on sentences that make it difficult to read and understand the main points.

Outcome:

- The client questions the professionalism of the proposal, leading to a lack of trust in the manager's competence.
- The manager learns the importance of proofreading and paying attention to grammar to maintain credibility and create a positive impression.

Structuring Business Documents

Importance of Structure and Organization:

The structure of business documents is critical for ensuring that the message is conveyed clearly and logically. Well-structured documents lead to clearer communication and better understanding.

- **Emails**: Should include a clear subject line, greeting, concise body, and closing. For instance, a subject line like *"Meeting Request: Q3 Performance Review"* immediately informs the recipient of the email's purpose.

- **Reports**: Should include essential sections such as a title page, table of contents, introduction, findings, conclusions, and recommendations. Each section plays a vital role in guiding the reader through the content.

- **Proposals**: Should have an executive summary, project overview, budget, and timeline, providing the recipient with all necessary information to make an informed decision.

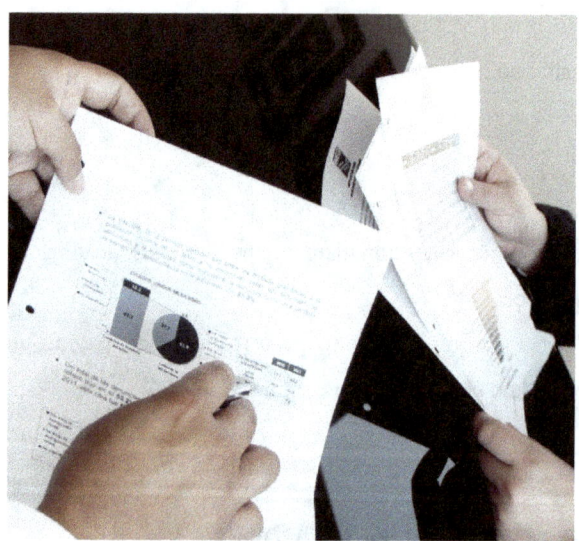

Writing Effective Business Emails

Key Elements of Business Emails:

- **Subject Line**: A specific and informative subject line sets the expectation for the content. For example, *"Follow-Up on Brainstorming Session - Next Steps"* is direct and tells the recipient what to expect.
- **Greeting**: Use appropriate salutations based on the relationship with the recipient. For formal communication, greetings like *"Dear Mr. Smith"* are ideal.
- **Body**: Be concise yet informative. Use bullet points for clarity when listing items or actions. Keeping the email focused ensures that the recipient can quickly understand the main message.
- **Closing Remarks**: End with a polite sign-off, such as *"Best regards"* or *"Sincerely,"* to leave a positive and professional impression.

Importance of Professionalism in Tone and Style:

- Maintain a respectful and courteous tone, avoid slang, and adapt the level of formality based on the recipient and the context.
- A professional tone establishes credibility, especially when communicating with clients, senior management, or external stakeholders.

The Art of Persuasion in Business Writing

Techniques for Persuasive Writing:

- **Understanding the Audience**: Knowing your audience's needs, preferences, and pain points helps in crafting a message that resonates with them.

- **Clear Messaging**: Be direct in articulating the benefits of your proposal or idea. Clarity increases the likelihood that the audience will see value in what you are presenting.

- **Strong Conclusions**: Conclude with a compelling call to action. For example, *"Let's schedule a follow-up meeting to discuss this further"* provides direction and encourages engagement.

Real-Life Scenario – The Art of Persuasion

Scenario Description:

A manager is pitching a new product line to potential investors, aiming to secure funding for an expansion.

Situation:

- The manager highlights customer pain points, presents relevant market research data, and crafts a narrative that explains how the new product addresses these needs effectively.
- By using compelling language that emphasizes benefits, such as *"This product will streamline processes, reduce costs, and ultimately drive growth,"* the manager captures the investors' interest.

Outcome:

- The persuasive language and well-structured presentation result in increased interest, with several investors expressing their willingness to discuss potential investment opportunities further.

Conclusion: Lessons from Real-Life Scenarios

Key Takeaways:

- Word power and grammar can have a significant impact on the effectiveness of communication in the workplace.

- Using precise vocabulary, maintaining proper grammar, and structuring documents clearly contribute to professionalism and influence in business settings.

- Continuous learning and vocabulary expansion are essential for developing effective communication skills that reflect leadership and competence.

By understanding and applying these principles, professionals can enhance their communication, foster stronger relationships, and achieve greater success in their careers.

Chapter Three:

Language and Structure Essentials for Business Communication

Effective communication in the business world transcends the mere selection of the right words; it hinges on the ability to construct sentences and paragraphs that convey ideas with clarity and professionalism. Business writing serves as the foundation for a variety of interactions—whether it be emails, reports, proposals, or presentations—and the quality of this writing can significantly influence perceptions, decisions, and outcomes.

However, many individuals encounter common challenges that can undermine the effectiveness of their written communication. These issues can range from ambiguous language and excessive jargon to unclear structures and grammatical errors. Such pitfalls not only obscure the intended message but also may lead to misunderstandings, decreased credibility, and lost opportunities.

In this chapter, we will explore these prevalent issues in business writing, providing insights into their origins and implications. More importantly, we will offer practical solutions that empower you to enhance the clarity and effectiveness of your communication. By addressing these common challenges, you will be better equipped to craft messages that resonate with your audience, convey professionalism, and facilitate informed decision-making. This journey towards improved business writing will not only bolster your individual communication skills but also contribute to the overall effectiveness of your organization.

I. Common Issues

1. Fragmented Sentences

Problem: A fragmented sentence is a group of words that has been broken off from the preceding or succeeding sentence, making it incomplete. This type of sentence lacks the essential components needed to convey a complete thought.

- **Example of Fragmented Sentences**:
  - *Even though I tried to fix the error.*
  - *Sarah said.*

To function as a complete sentence, it must contain:

1. A **subject** (the person or thing performing an action).
2. A **predicate** (the action or what is being said about the subject).
3. A **complete thought** that can stand alone.

Solution: Make sure each sentence contains a subject and a predicate, and expresses a complete idea.

- **Incorrect**: *An apartment that was within walking distance of his job.*
- **Correct**: *Jack found an apartment that was within walking distance of his job.*

By adding a subject and verb, the sentence now stands alone as a complete thought.

2. Split Sentences and Comma Splices

Problem: A comma splice occurs when two independent clauses (complete sentences) are joined incorrectly with a comma.

- **Example of Comma Splice**:
  ○ *Susie went to the retail store, she wanted to find the Merchandising Manager.*
  ○ **Problem**: These are two separate clauses that cannot be joined by just a comma.

  Solution: Separate the clauses with a period, semicolon, or a conjunction.

- **Corrected**:
  ○ *Susie went to the retail store. She wanted to find the Merchandising Manager.*
  ○ Or use a semicolon if the thoughts are closely related: *Susie went to the retail store; she wanted to find the Merchandising Manager.*

  Use of Semi-Colons:

- **Connecting Related Independent Clauses**: *Martha has gone to the library; Andrew has gone to play soccer.*
- **Replacing Conjunctions**: *The fish tasted awful; the steak didn't taste good either.*

Semi-colons are effective in linking closely related ideas and adding variety to sentence structure.

3. Run-On Sentences

Problem: A run-on sentence occurs when different thoughts are joined together without proper punctuation or conjunctions.

- **Example**: *Employees want to keep their jobs they will work hard for promotions.*

  Solution: Break up the sentence into separate thoughts or add punctuation where needed.

- **Corrected**: *Employees want to keep their jobs. They will work hard for promotions.*

4. Unparallel Structures

Problem: Equal thoughts in a sentence should be expressed using the same grammatical structure. Unparallel structures can confuse readers and reduce the clarity of your message.

- **Incorrect**: *I like singing, dancing, and play basketball.*
- **Correct**: *I like singing, dancing, and playing basketball.*

Parallel structure ensures that similar elements are presented in a consistent format, enhancing readability and flow.

5. Plurals of Nouns

Usage:

- **Member** (singular) vs. **Members** (plural).
- The word **staff** can be singular (individual member) or collective (a group of staff).
- **Staff** (singular): *A staff member from the sales department.*
- **Staff** (collective, plural): *A group of staff in the sales department.*
- **Staffs** (plural): Used to refer to multiple groups of staff. *Staffs from the two departments are collaborating on this project.*

II. Word Choices in Reports & Proposals

Choosing the right words in reports and proposals is crucial to ensure that the message is professional, clear, and impactful.

Word Choices in Business Reports and Proposals

Reports:

Reports are written documents designed to communicate information about a specific subject.

Proposals:

Proposals aim to communicate information about a product, service, or idea in order to persuade the reader to adopt a recommended solution.

Tips for Effective Writing:

- **Understand the Reader**: Tailor the language to the intended audience to ensure clarity and engagement.
- **Use a Concise, Professional Style**: Avoid unnecessary jargon and keep the tone objective and factual.
- **Support Statements with Factual Information**: Use data, evidence, charts, and graphs to validate your claims.

Language of Reports and Proposals:

- When presenting **findings** in reports, it is common to:
1. Use **language of approximation** to describe numbers (e.g., *The annual revenue is approximately $1 million*).
2. Describe trends using appropriate verbs and nouns.

Language of Approximation in Reports and Proposals

Advantages:

- Numbers in reports often do not need to be exact unless required for specific purposes.
- **Example**: *The annual revenue is around $1 million* is often sufficient unless the exact number is critical.
- If readers need precise figures, they can refer to tables, charts, and graphs provided in the report.

Examples of Approximate Language:

- **10% of sales**: *A tenth of the sales volume.*
- **25% of sales**: *A quarter of the sales volume.*
- **50% of staff**: *Half of the staff.*
- **$1,010,000**: *Over a million dollars.*

Language of Approximation - Dos and Don'ts

DOs:

- Add an 's' to fractions starting with two or greater (e.g., *two-thirds*).
- Use plural nouns after fractions (e.g., *half of the books*).
- Use terms like *just* and *only* to imply limitations (e.g., *Only 5% of staff were promoted*).

DON'Ts:

- Do not begin a sentence with Arabic numerals (e.g., use *Ten employees* instead of *10 employees*).
- Avoid using fractions with denominators greater than five, as they are harder for most people to understand.
- Remember to include a hyphen in fractions (e.g., *one-tenth*).

Describing Trends in Graphs and Reports

Describing trends is essential when presenting data in reports and proposals. Using precise language to describe changes ensures clarity and provides valuable insights to the reader.

Describing Trends Generally Includes Three Parts:

1. **Describe the Movement**: Use appropriate verbs or nouns.
2. **Describe the Speed or Size of the Movement**: Use adjectives or adverbs.
3. **Explain the Reason or Consequence of the Change**.

Example: *In 2021, Apple's profits increased considerably thanks to its successful iPhone 12 series.*

1. Describe the Movement Using a Verb

Upward Movement (Verbs):

- To **climb**
- To **reach a peak**
- To **rise** (past tense: rose)
- To **increase**
- To **recover**
- To **rocket** (for significant increases)

Downward Movement (Verbs):

- To **fall** (past tense: fell)
- To **decline**
- To **drop**
- To **plummet** (for significant drops)
- To **decrease**

Horizontal Movement (Verbs):

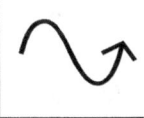

- To **remain stable**
- To **level off**
- To **stabilize**
- To **fluctuate** (for irregular changes)

2. Describe the Movement Using a Noun

Upward Movement (Nouns):

- **Growth**
- **Rise**
- **Increase**
- **Peak**

Downward Movement (Nouns):

- **Decline**
- **Decrease**
- **Dip** (a temporary drop)
- **Drop**

Horizontal Movement (Nouns):

- **Stability**
- **Fluctuation**

3. Describe the Speed or Size of the Movement

To accurately convey the magnitude or speed of a trend, use adjectives and adverbs.

- **Adjective + Noun**: *There was a significant increase in sales figures.*
- **Verb + Adverb**: *Sales figures increased steadily.*

Examples:

- *The sales of ABC Company increased dramatically between 2024 and 2025.*
- *There was a rapid decline in sales from 2022 to 2023.*
- *Sales remained stable at $3 million in 2022.*

Explaining the Reason or Consequence of the Change

To explain why a trend has occurred or what its impact is, use appropriate linking phrases.

Useful Expressions:

1. **As a result of** (noun)…
o *As a result of the COVID-19 outbreak, sales dropped significantly in 2021.*
2. **Due to** (noun)…
o *Due to changes in export policy, sales dipped dramatically in 2021.*
3. **Because of** (noun)…
o *Because of increased competition, market share declined.*
4. **(Noun) caused (noun)**…
o *The new marketing campaign caused an increase in customer engagement.*
5. **Consequently**…
o *The product launch was delayed. Consequently, sales targets were not met.*

Conclusion

Understanding the common issues in business writing and the essentials of language structure is crucial for effective communication. By recognizing fragmented sentences, run-ons, and parallel structure problems, you can significantly improve the quality of your writing. Choosing the right words and understanding how to describe trends clearly and effectively can help convey your message to stakeholders, clients, and team members in a professional manner. Mastering these skills is a key step toward becoming an effective business communicator.

Chapter Four:

Fundamentals of Business Writing

In the fast-paced world of business, the ability to communicate effectively through writing is invaluable. In this chapter, we will delve into the essentials of effective business writing, placing special emphasis on two fundamental types of business documents: reports and proposals. These essential documents play crucial roles in conveying information, persuading stakeholders, and facilitating decision-making.

To master these forms of communication, we will discuss a structured approach that outlines the critical components of crafting clear and impactful reports and proposals. We will examine the three key writing stages—planning, drafting, and revising—which serve as a framework for ensuring that your documents meet the highest standards of clarity and engagement.

- **Report Writing**: This segment will focus on the structured approach needed for effective report writing. We will explore how to convey complex information and analysis systematically, aiding the reader's understanding and facilitating informed decision-making.
- **Proposal Writing**: Here, we will address the art of crafting persuasive proposals. Proposals are not just documents; they are strategic tools designed to outline projects and secure approval. We will discuss techniques for making a compelling case that resonates with stakeholders and prompts action.
- **Writing Stages**: Lastly, we will delve into the vital writing stages of planning, drafting, and revising. Each of these stages is essential for enhancing the clarity, accuracy, and overall impact of your business communications.

By the end of this chapter, you will have a comprehensive understanding of how to approach business writing effectively, enabling you to produce professional documents that fulfill their intended purpose and engage your audience persuasively.

What is a Report?

Definition: A **report** is an orderly and objective document that serves a specific purpose after investigating a situation or event. It is created in accordance with certain requirements, often based on research or analysis, and provides insights or recommendations.

Channels ("Modes"):

- Reports can be delivered in both **written** and **oral** formats.
- They can take the form of a **letter**, **memo**, or a formal report, depending on the intended audience and purpose.

Three Characteristics of Reports

1. **Upward Flow**: Reports often travel upward within an organization, requested by management or higher authorities for the purpose of decision-making.

2. **Objectivity**: Reports underscore the need for objectivity, as they contribute to decision-making and problem-solving. A report should be factual and unbiased to maintain its credibility.

3. **Audience Specificity**: Reports are typically tailored for a specific audience, especially when circulated within an organization. To enhance objectivity, minimize the use of personal pronouns:
   - Instead of '*I recommend that...*', use '*It is suggested that...*'.
   - Replace '*It is recommended that...*' with '*The recommendation is that...*'.

Functions and Types of Reports

When to Use Reports

- **Sales Report**: Outlines the quantity of goods or services sold and explains discrepancies from projected figures.

- **Progress Report**: Details the status of a project, assessing progress towards completion.

- **Incident Report**: Provides an account of an event that has occurred, such as accidents or unexpected occurrences.

- **Feasibility Report**: Evaluates the practicality of a proposal, including its potential risks and benefits.

- **Recommendation Report**: Suggests appropriate actions based on research and analysis.

- **Accident Report**: Details how injuries were sustained or how items were damaged, often used for insurance or liability purposes.

Business Proposals

A **business proposal** is a formal document that presents a solution to a specific business problem or opportunity. It aims to convince a potential client or investor of the value of the proposed product, service, or project.

Characteristics of a Business Proposal:

- **Problem-Solving Focus**: A proposal identifies a problem and offers a detailed solution.

- **Structured Format**: A proposal follows a consistent structure, including an executive summary, a statement of the problem, a proposed solution, and a conclusion.

- **Persuasive Nature**: Proposals use persuasive language to convince the reader that the proposed solution is the best choice.

Solicited vs. Unsolicited Proposals

Solicited Proposals:

- Initiated in response to a formal **Request for Proposal (RFP)** issued by an organization.
- Example: The Hong Kong SAR government invites interested parties to propose solutions for a food truck initiative. Guidelines and formats are provided to structure responses.

Unsolicited Proposals:

- Similar to a sales letter, these proposals are not requested but aim to persuade a potential client or partner of an opportunity.
- More flexible in formatting and content.

Examples of Business Proposals

1. Sales Proposal for a Marketing Agency:

- *Executive Summary*: Proposes a comprehensive marketing campaign for XYZ Corporation's new product, focusing on digital marketing and strategic planning. The campaign aims to increase brand awareness and drive sales through targeted online advertising, engaging social media content, and promotional materials.

2. Grant Proposal for a Non-Profit Organization:

- *Executive Summary*: Proposes an arts education program for underserved youth, including workshops, classes, and mentorship opportunities led by experienced artists. The program aims to enhance cultural skills and provide valuable life experiences.

3. Investment Proposal for a Tech Startup:

- *Executive Summary*: Proposes investment in a mobile payment app that provides secure, convenient transactions. The app uses encryption and biometric authentication for safety, aiming to scale user growth with strategic marketing.

4. Partnership Proposal between Two Companies:

- *Executive Summary*: Proposes a partnership between two companies to develop and market a new line of innovative products, leveraging each company's strengths and expertise.

5. Government Contract Proposal:

- *Executive Summary*: Proposes highway maintenance services for the Department of Transportation, detailing a comprehensive plan for road repairs, pavement marking, and bridge maintenance, emphasizing efficiency and quality.

Overview: The Three-Step Business Writing Process

Successful business writing follows a structured process to ensure quality, clarity, and effectiveness. The three steps are:

1. **Planning**: Establishing the purpose, understanding the audience, and gathering necessary information.
2. **Drafting**: Writing the first version, focusing on content rather than perfection.
3. **Revising**: Reviewing and improving clarity, organization, and impact.

The Planning Stage

The planning stage is critical for setting a strong foundation for the document.

1. **Setting the Writing Objective**
   o Be **audience-centered**: Focus on what the audience needs to know.
   o Define a specific **target audience** and have a clear desired response from them.
   o Determine an **accomplishment date** or relevant details to help set expectations.
   o **Example Objective**: *As a result of the meeting, staff will observe the new dress code effective from April 1, 2025.*

2. **Analyzing Your Audience**
   o Understand the **audience size and composition**. Tailor the message accordingly:
   ▪ **Primary Audience**: The main decision-makers, such as the Board of Directors deciding on a merger.
   ▪ **Initial Audience**: Those who receive the document first and may forward it, such as project managers or assistants.
   ▪ **Secondary Audience**: Individuals who are indirectly affected, like HR or finance teams.

   ▪ **Gatekeeper**: A person controlling the flow of information, such as a legal advisor or IT manager.

- **Watchdog**: External parties monitoring compliance, such as auditors or consumer rights organizations.

3. **Adapting the Message to the Audience**
   o Tailor the language, style, and tone based on the audience's preferences and familiarity with the subject. For technical audiences, precise terms may be necessary, whereas for broader audiences, simplicity is key.

Communication Channels

Selecting the appropriate **communication channel** is crucial for effective message delivery:

- **Written Reports**: Formal documents that provide detailed information.
- **Presentations**: Ideal for engaging a group, allowing for real-time interaction and feedback.
- **Emails**: Useful for concise communication, especially for following up or summarizing key points.

The Drafting and Revising stage

Drafting involves writing the initial version of the report or proposal, where the focus is on getting ideas down without worrying too much about language precision or grammar.

Revising is a crucial step where the document is reviewed and refined for:

- **Clarity**: Ensuring the message is easy to understand.
- **Engagement**: Using techniques such as rhetorical questions or examples to engage the reader.
- **Conciseness**: Removing unnecessary words or redundancy.

The Writing Stage

The final stage of business writing that follows planning, drafting, and revising represents a critical juncture—a synthesis of strategic insight and meticulous craftsmanship designed not just to convey information, but to forge connections and drive action in the intricate landscape of the professional world.

At this point, the writer morphs into a strategic communicator, understanding that the nuances of language can hold significant power in business interactions. Each sentence becomes a carefully considered decision point, honed not only for grammatical accuracy but for its potential impact on the reader. The focus sharpens on clarity—a hallmark of effective business writing—ensuring that even the most complex ideas are distilled into straightforward, digestible formats. The writer expresses concepts with precision, minimizing jargon unless it serves a purpose that adds clarity to the message.

This stage is characterized by a heightened awareness of audience dynamics; the writer embodies an empathetic perspective, striving to anticipate the questions, interests, and potential objections of the reader. It is essential to tailor the message to resonate with varied stakeholders, whether they are executives, team members, clients, or potential partners. This nuanced understanding of the audience shifts the writing beyond mere information dissemination to an engaging dialogue that invites participation and fosters understanding.

In the world of business writing, tone plays a pivotal role. The prosperity of a company often hinges on careful choices of tone—assertive yet respectful, decisive yet open to dialogue. This is where the writer calibrates their approach, considering the nature of the communication. A compelling proposal may require a tone that is confident and optimistic, while a sensitive email addressing a miscommunication would necessitate a more conciliatory and understanding demeanor. Striking the right balance ensures that the message is received in the spirit it was intended, building trust and rapport between parties.

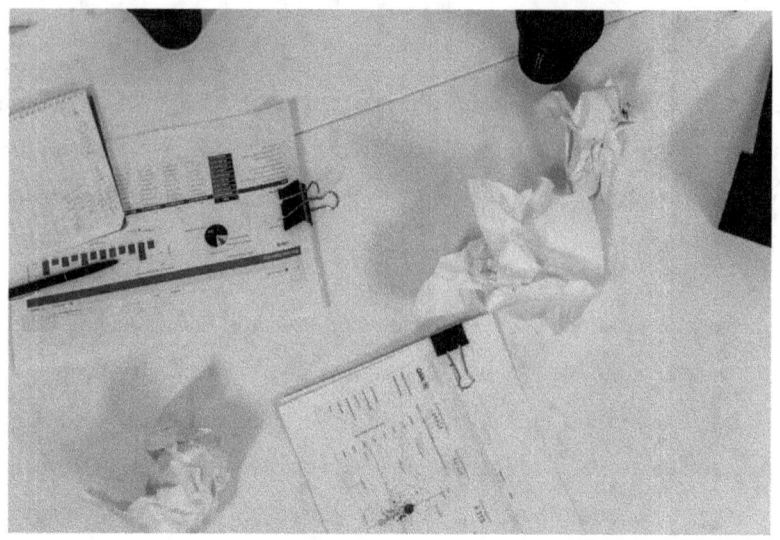

As the writer perfects their words, they also attend to the visual elements of the document, recognizing that presentation can greatly influence perception. A well-formatted document, with clear headings, bullet points, and visual aids such as charts or infographics, enhances readability and engages the reader's attention. Effective business writing acknowledges that people process information differently, and incorporating visuals can help clarify complex data and concepts, making them more accessible and memorable.

The iterative process of revision comes into sharp focus during this phase. It is not merely about correcting typographical errors but ensuring that every word serves a purpose and contributes to the overall effectiveness of the communication. The writer may solicit feedback from peers or stakeholders, understanding that collaboration can illuminate blind spots and lead to more refined ideas. Each round of revisions should bring the piece closer to perfection, resulting in a document that is polished, professional, and powerful in its intent.

Ultimately, this final stage of business writing transforms the document from a collection of ideas into a strategic communication vehicle—ready to inform, persuade, or motivate the intended audience. It stands as a testament to the writer's commitment to quality, reflecting not just their own standards but those of the organization they represent. In a competitive business environment, effective writing can be a distinct advantage, facilitating clear communication, building relationships, and ultimately driving successful outcomes.

The culmination of planning, drafting, and revising fosters a piece that not only conveys information but does so in a way that engages and influences its readers, transforming them into allies or informed decision-makers in the business narrative.

Conclusion

Mastering the fundamentals of business writing—whether for reports or proposals—requires a structured approach that emphasizes planning, audience analysis, and clarity. Reports aim to present information objectively, aiding in decision-making, while proposals are persuasive documents designed to convince the reader of a specific course of action. By applying these principles, business professionals can communicate more effectively, enhancing both individual and organizational success.

Chapter Five:

Persuasive Writing in Business

Persuasion is the strategic art of influencing the beliefs, attitudes, intentions, or actions of stakeholders through tailored communication. In the realm of business, effective persuasion is not merely about presenting information; it involves thoughtfully framing messages to resonate with the audience's values, needs, and objectives. The ultimate aim is to motivate action or inspire changes in perception.

Persuasion plays a critical role in various business interactions, from negotiating deals and securing funding to gaining buy-in for new initiatives and fostering customer loyalty. It requires an understanding of not only the content of the message but also the nuances of the audience's mindset. Crafting persuasive communication involves several key elements, including clarity, relevance, emotional appeal, and credibility.

In this chapter, we will explore the essential components of persuasive communication, examining techniques for effectively engaging an audience and influencing their decisions. We will also consider ethical implications, ensuring that persuasion is conducted with integrity and respect for stakeholder perspectives. By mastering the art of persuasion, you will enhance your ability to drive meaningful conversations, facilitate cooperation, and achieve desired outcomes within your business environment.

Theoretical Foundation:

Persuasion draws from both classical and modern theories. **Aristotle's rhetoric** emphasizes the importance of ethos (credibility), pathos (emotional appeal), and logos (logic). Modern frameworks such as the **Elaboration Likelihood Model (ELM)** illustrate how the level of audience engagement influences the effectiveness of persuasive messages. ELM distinguishes between two routes: the **central route**, where deep processing occurs, and the **peripheral route**, where superficial cues influence decisions.

Purpose in Business:

Effective persuasion is vital for driving decisions—whether it's convincing stakeholders to approve projects, motivating teams to embrace new initiatives, or persuading clients to purchase a product. Mastering persuasive techniques enhances the ability to create compelling business proposals or impactful presentations that resonate with the target audience.

Aristotle's Rhetorical Triangle: Ethos, Pathos, Logos

Aristotle's classical model of persuasion is based on three essential elements used to craft persuasive arguments.

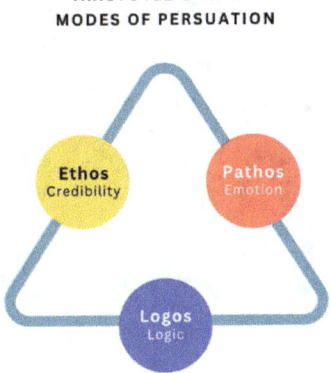

Ethos (Credibility and Ethical Appeal): Establishes the speaker's trustworthiness and authority.

- **Example**: An experienced financial advisor shares their expertise, stating, *"With over 15 years of managing portfolios, I can assure you that this strategy is sound for long-term growth."*

Pathos (Emotional Appeal): Engages the audience's emotions to elicit a response.

- **Example**: A charity highlights a personal story of someone in need, saying, *"Every child deserves to go to bed with a full stomach and hope for a better tomorrow."*

Logos (Logical Appeal): Relies on facts, data, and logical reasoning to persuade.

- **Example**: A business analyst presents a report showing that sales increased by 30% after implementing a new marketing strategy, thus proving the campaign's effectiveness.

Cialdini's Six Principles of Persuasion

Dr. Robert Cialdini (1984), an expert in the psychology of influence, identified six key principles that guide human behavior and can be used to craft persuasive business messages.

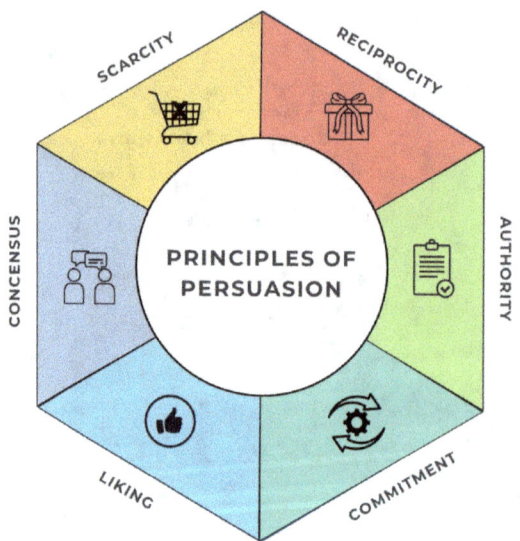

1. **Reciprocity**: People feel compelled to return favors.
   - **Example**: Offering a free consultation often encourages the client to reciprocate by considering your services.
2. **Commitment and Consistency**: People prefer to act consistently with previous commitments.
   - **Example**: After getting a verbal agreement from a client, follow up with a proposal that aligns with their prior commitment.

3. **Social Proof**: People tend to follow the actions of others.
o **Example**: Highlighting testimonials or case studies from satisfied clients can build trust and influence potential customers.
4. **Authority**: People respect those in positions of authority or expertise.
o **Example**: Including credentials and endorsements from industry experts can boost the credibility of your proposal.
5. **Liking**: People are more likely to agree with individuals they like or relate to.
o **Example**: Establishing rapport through shared interests or values can make your audience more receptive to your message.
6. **Scarcity**: People value things that are perceived as rare or limited.
o **Example**: Emphasizing that an offer is available for a limited time can create urgency and prompt faster decision-making.

Key Elements of Persuasive Structure

A structured approach to persuasion helps organize messages effectively. **Monroe's Motivated Sequence** is a well-known framework that guides persuasive communication in five stages (Monroe, 1943):

1. **Attention**: Grab the audience's attention with a strong opening.
2. **Need**: Describe the problem that requires a solution.
3. **Satisfaction**: Present a solution that meets the need.
4. **Visualization**: Help the audience visualize the benefits of the solution.
5. **Action**: Provide a clear and specific call to action.

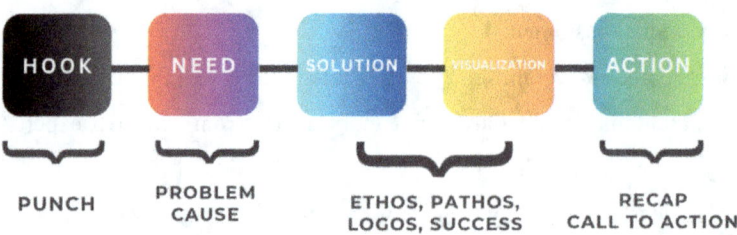

THE MOTIVATED SEQUENCE

| HOOK | NEED | SOLUTION | VISUALIZATION | ACTION |

PUNCH | PROBLEM CAUSE | ETHOS, PATHOS, LOGOS, SUCCESS | RECAP CALL TO ACTION

Example: In a recent company meeting, an HR manager presented a proposal for a wellness program. She began by sharing alarming statistics about employee burnout (**Attention**), explained its impact on productivity (**Need**), introduced a wellness program as a solution (**Satisfaction**), described a healthier workplace (**Visualization**), and ended with a request for support to launch the initiative (**Action**).

Writing Persuasive Introductions

Goal: Craft an introduction that captures attention and piques interest immediately.

Theoretical Insight: The **Primacy Effect** suggests that people are most likely to remember the first information they receive. A strong introduction ensures that the initial impression is impactful.

- **Example**: Starting a proposal with, *"By implementing this strategy, we can increase profits by 15% within six months,"* immediately gives the reader a reason to be interested.

Developing the Body of a Persuasive Document

The Art of Persuasion: Constructing a Compelling Argument

In the realm of business writing, the ability to persuade is a crucial skill, particularly when crafting documents intended to sway opinions, influence decisions, or inspire action. At the heart of any persuasive document lies a well-developed body that serves not only to articulate the central idea but to do so in a manner that resonates with the audience. To achieve this, writers must meticulously weave together logical reasoning, emotional appeal, and credibility, creating a compelling argument that captures attention and fosters conviction.

Logical Reasoning: The Backbone of Persuasion

First and foremost, logical reasoning forms the backbone of a persuasive argument. It involves presenting ideas that are coherent and follow a structured thought process, allowing the audience to understand and accept the argument being made. This can take the form of deductive or inductive reasoning.

Deductive reasoning starts with a general principle or premise and works its way down to a specific conclusion. For example, a business proposal might begin with the premise that *"increased investments in employee training lead to higher productivity,"* followed by supporting data and a conclusion that recommends enhancing training programs to boost overall efficiency. Conversely, inductive reasoning moves from specific examples to broader generalizations. By presenting evidence from case studies or data, a writer can lead the audience to draw wider implications from those examples, engaging them in a way that appears rational and well-founded.

In addition to structured reasoning, it is essential that logical reasoning is underpinned by relevant data, statistics, and factual evidence. Citing reputable sources adds weight to the argument, enabling the writer to present their case convincingly. For instance, if advocating for a new marketing strategy, incorporating data showing measurable success from comparable organizations can significantly bolster the argument. By aligning claims with empirical evidence, the writer can create an irrefutable foundation that caters to an audience focused on logic and rationality.

Emotional Appeal: Connecting with the Audience

While logical reasoning is critical, it is not the sole component of a persuasive argument. Emotional appeal—often referred to as pathos—plays a vital role in engaging the audience on a deeper level. Human beings do not solely operate on a logical basis; they are motivated, swayed, and often moved by emotions. Thus, a persuasive document must resonate emotionally with its audience to create a lasting impact.

To evoke emotional responses, writers can utilize storytelling techniques, illustrating their points through relatable anecdotes. For example, when arguing for a workplace wellness program, recounting the story of an employee who benefitted from such a program can humanize the statistics, portraying a narrative that the audience can empathize with. This connection fosters a sense of urgency or concern, prompting readers to care about the issue at hand.

Additionally, employing evocative language can stir feelings of excitement, fear, hope, or even indignation. Through carefully selected words and phrases, a writer can paint a picture that allows the audience to feel the weight of the argument. The challenge lies in ensuring that emotional appeal does not overshadow logical reasoning; instead, it should complement and enhance it, creating a more holistic and persuasive argument.

Credibility: Establishing Trust and Authority

The third pillar of a persuasive document is credibility, or ethos—the trustworthiness and authority of the writer. Establishing credibility is crucial, as an argument loses power if the audience doubts the writer's integrity or expertise. To bolster credibility, writers should not only demonstrate knowledge of the subject matter but also acknowledge counterarguments and address them appropriately.

Presenting oneself as knowledgeable includes thorough research and familiarity with the topic at hand. Incorporating expert testimonials, citing reputable studies, and utilizing data from credible sources convey a sense of authority. Additionally, it is helpful to outline the writer's qualifications or experiences that relate to the topic, thereby enhancing trustworthiness. When readers perceive the writer as an expert, they are more likely to accept the arguments presented.

However, credibility also hinges on the writer's ethical stance. Persuasive writing should strive to be honest and transparent, avoiding misleading statistics or overstated claims. Acknowledging opposing viewpoints—often treated as areas of concern by the audience—can show that the writer is considerate and well-rounded in their thinking, further establishing trust. By articulating potential downsides while reiterating the benefits, the argument can appear more balanced and fair-minded, increasing the likelihood of acceptance.

The Synergy of Reasoning, Emotion, and Credibility

When these three elements—logical reasoning, emotional appeal, and credibility—are effectively woven together, they create a powerful persuasive narrative. Each component reinforces the others, forming a cohesive tapestry that engages the audience's intellect and emotions alike. A compelling argument captures not just the mind but the heart, forging connections that drive readers to consider and, ideally, act upon the ideas presented.

In conclusion, crafting a persuasive document is a nuanced art that involves a deep understanding of one's audience and the strategic integration of logical reasoning, emotional appeal, and credibility. By developing arguments thoroughly and deliberately, writers can create persuasive pieces that not only inform but inspire decisive action and foster change in the business landscape. The success of these documents hinges not only on what is said but how it is articulated, making the mastery of persuasion an invaluable skill in professional communication.

Theoretical Insight: **Cognitive Dissonance Theory** explains that people feel discomfort when their beliefs or actions are inconsistent. A persuasive argument can resolve this discomfort by aligning the proposed solution with the audience's existing beliefs.

- **Example**: In a proposal, anticipate potential objections—such as cost concerns—and counter them by demonstrating the long-term financial benefits of the proposal. This helps resolve the reader's cognitive dissonance.

Writing Persuasive Conclusions

Theory: The **Recency Effect** suggests that people are likely to remember the last information presented to them.

Goal: Reinforce key messages and provide a strong call to action that prompts the desired response.

- **Example**: *"Implementing this solution will improve efficiency by 25%. Let's set up a meeting next week to discuss the next steps."*
- **Example**: *"I recommend we move forward with this proposal immediately to capitalize on emerging market opportunities."*

The Importance of Clarity and Brevity

Cognitive Load Theory states that people can only process a limited amount of information at a time. Overloading your audience with too much information can result in confusion and decreased persuasion effectiveness.

Best Practices:

- Use simple, direct language.
- Break complex ideas into bullet points or numbered lists to enhance readability.

- **Example**: Instead of presenting a dense paragraph, simplify it with bullet points that clearly outline key benefits.

Using Evidence and Data

People tend to favor information that confirms their existing beliefs (**Confirmation Bias**). Presenting data that aligns with the audience's values or priorities can increase the persuasiveness of your message.

- **Example**: Citing industry research that supports your proposed solution can bolster credibility and align with the reader's expectations.
- **Example**: Including case studies demonstrating successful outcomes reinforces your argument's validity.

Framing Your Argument

The **Framing Effect** refers to how the presentation of information affects decision-making. How you frame your argument can significantly impact how it is received.

- **Positive Frame**: Highlight the potential gains.
  o **Example**: *"Adopting this strategy will open up new market opportunities and boost profits."*
- **Negative Frame**: Emphasize potential risks of inaction.
  o **Example**: *"Failing to implement this solution could lead to missed opportunities and loss of market share."*

Common Mistakes in Persuasive Writing

Mistakes to Avoid:

- **Vagueness**: A lack of specific details weakens the argument.
- Example: Avoid statements like *"This will improve efficiency."* Instead, specify by how much and in what way.

- **Overloading with Details**: Providing too much information can be overwhelming and dilute the key message.
- Example: Instead of a long-winded explanation, summarize key points concisely.

- **No Clear Call to Action**: The audience must know exactly what is expected of them.
- Example: Always conclude with a specific, actionable step, such as *"Schedule a meeting to discuss the next phase."*

Best Practices for Persuasive Writing

Tips:

- **Stay Focused**: Keep the content aligned with your primary goal.
- **Use an Active Voice**: Active sentences are more direct and engaging.
- **Provide Evidence**: Use data, testimonials, or examples to back up your claims.
- **Include a Clear Call to Action**: Make sure the audience knows what action to take next.

Chapter Six:

Bridging Cultures: Mastering Cross-Cultural Communication

In an era characterized by rapid globalization and interconnectedness, the ability to communicate effectively across cultural boundaries has never been more crucial. As we embark on this exploration of cultural dimensions and their profound impact on communication, we will uncover the intricate ways in which diverse cultural frameworks shape our interactions. Each culture possesses its own set of values, beliefs, and communication styles, all of which influence the manner in which messages are delivered and interpreted. As we delve into these cultural dimensions, we'll not only gain insight into the foundational elements that inform our communication but also learn to recognize potential pitfalls that can arise from misunderstandings.

Adapting persuasive techniques to fit various cultural contexts stands as a vital skill in this landscape. What resonates strongly with one audience may fall flat or, worse, offend another, making it essential for communicators to tailor their messages to reflect the unique characteristics of the cultures they engage with. This chapter will guide you through the nuances of persuasive communication across cultures, providing you with strategies to identify cultural preferences and expectations. The aim is to equip you with the tools necessary to craft messages that are not only impactful but also respectful and culturally appropriate.

Moreover, as we navigate the complexities of cross-cultural interactions, developing effective strategies for managing these encounters will be critical. This entails more than mere awareness of differences; it requires proactive engagement, active listening, and the courage to embrace new perspectives. We will explore practical techniques that emphasize empathy and adaptability, allowing you to foster an environment conducive to open dialogue. By recognizing and valuing the rich tapestry of cultural diversity, we can mitigate conflicts and enhance understanding, laying the groundwork for more meaningful connections.

As we progress through this chapter and beyond, the objective is clear: to cultivate a comprehensive understanding of cultural dimensions in communication and empower you to navigate the intricate web of human interactions with confidence, respect, and insight. Let us embark on this journey to enrich our communication skills, embracing the beauty of diversity as we learn to connect more effectively with the world around us.

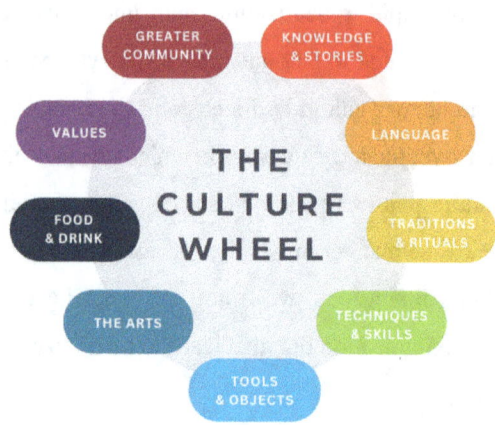

Defining Culture in Business

Culture, fundamentally defined, encompasses the shared **values, norms, beliefs**, and behaviors that characterize a particular group or society. These components intricately shape how individuals within those cultures perceive the world and interact with one another, laying the groundwork for their social and business practices. The impact of cultural differences on business operations can be profound, influencing everything from decision-making processes to interpersonal interactions. For instance, organizations operating internationally must navigate these cultural variations to foster effective collaboration and avoid miscommunication.

A compelling example of this can be seen in IKEA, which has successfully adapted its product lines and marketing strategies to align with local cultural preferences. While the brand originally embodies the essence of Scandinavian minimalism, it has made significant adjustments to appeal to diverse markets, such as in the Middle East. In these regions, IKEA has reconfigured its offerings to incorporate local traditions and preferences, adapting everything from design aesthetics to functionality, all while ensuring that its core brand identity remains intact. This adaptability not only demonstrates the importance of cultural understanding in business but also highlights how thoughtful engagement with local customs can enhance a company's success in the global marketplace.

Cultural Dimensions and Their Influence on Persuasion

Hofstede's Cultural Dimensions Theory (1980) and Persuasion

Overview of Hofstede's Dimensions: Geert Hofstede developed six key cultural dimensions to explain cultural differences and how they influence behavior:

- **Power Distance**: Acceptance of unequal power distribution.
- **Individualism vs. Collectivism**: Focus on individual goals vs. group goals.
- **Masculinity vs. Femininity**: Value placed on competition, assertiveness vs. care, and quality of life.
- **Uncertainty Avoidance**: Comfort with ambiguity and risk.
- **Long-Term Orientation**: Focus on future rewards vs. short-term results.
- **Indulgence**: Allowing free gratification of desires vs. control over desires.

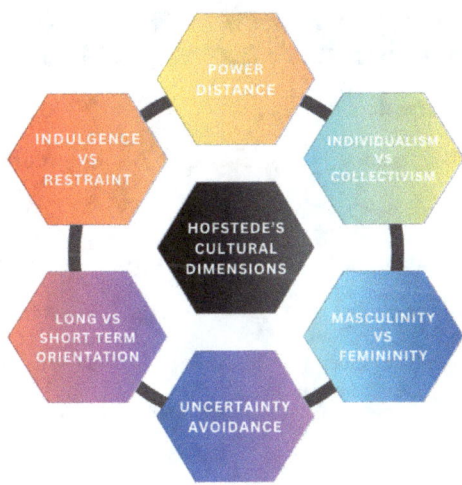

Influence on Persuasion:

- **High Power Distance Cultures** (e.g., Russia) tend to respond positively to authority figures and hierarchical structures. Using authoritative language or referring to experts may enhance persuasiveness.
- **Low Power Distance Cultures** (e.g., Sweden) prefer participative decision-making, and persuasive messages should emphasize **consensus-building** and teamwork.

Example: When persuading employees in **Russia** (high Power Distance), an approach that emphasizes respect for authority and decisions from senior management is likely to be effective. In contrast, persuading employees in **Sweden** (low Power Distance) works better when emphasizing shared goals and collective decision-making.

Trompenaars' Seven Dimensions of Culture (1997) and Audience Analysis

Trompenaars' Model: Trompenaars and Hampden-Turner introduced seven cultural dimensions, including:

- **Universalism vs. Particularism**: Universal rules vs. relationship-based decisions.
- **Achievement vs. Ascription**: Status based on achievements vs. status based on who you are.

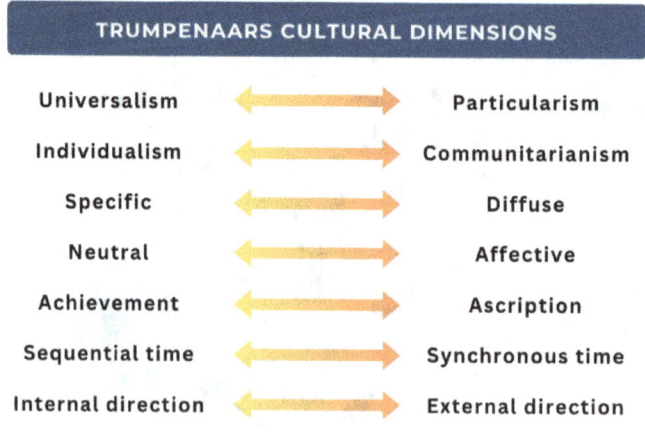

Influence on Persuasion:

- In **Particularist Cultures** (e.g., Brazil), relationship-building is essential for persuasion. Establishing trust and demonstrating commitment can be more persuasive than a purely logical argument.
- In **Universalist Cultures** (e.g., Switzerland), fairness and adherence to rules are crucial, so persuasion relies more on presenting **objective facts** and consistency.

Example: Persuading a client in **Brazil** may involve spending time to build rapport and emphasizing shared values, while persuading a client in **Switzerland** would focus on presenting well-structured data and ensuring fairness.

Lewis Model of Cultural Types (1996) and Message Framing

Lewis Model: The Lewis Model categorizes cultures into three types based on their communication style and approach to tasks:

- **Linear-active**: Task-oriented, highly organized, and prefer logical communication.
- **Multi-active**: People-oriented, prefer emotional and engaging communication.
- **Reactive**: Focus on listening, harmonizing, and indirect communication.

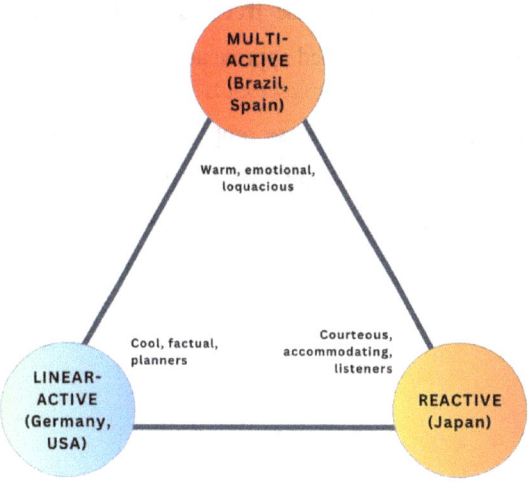

Communication Styles Across Cultures and Persuasive Techniques

Identifying High-Context vs. Low-Context Communication – Deep Dive

High-Context Cultures:

- Often use **peripheral cues** in communication, such as **body language**, **symbolism**, and **tone**. Persuasion relies on building relationships and shared meanings.

Low-Context Cultures:

- Prefer **central route cues** such as **direct argumentation** and explicit reasoning. Persuasion involves presenting logical arguments and factual data.

Example: A business presentation for a **Saudi Arabian** audience (high-context) may involve indirect language and emphasis on relationships, whereas a presentation for an **Australian** audience (low-context) would involve direct, fact-based communication.

Negotiation Styles and Persuasive Techniques

Direct vs. Indirect Negotiation Styles:

- **Direct Cultures** (e.g., U.S., Germany) prefer clear, unambiguous language and logical arguments (**logos**).
- **Indirect Cultures** (e.g., Japan, Thailand) value subtlety, empathy, and relationship-building, often favoring emotional appeals (**pathos**).

Example: An **American negotiator** might present a detailed list of benefits and costs, while **Japanese negotiator** might emphasize long-term relationships and mutual benefits.

Writing for a Global Audience with Persuasive Intent

Adapting Persuasive Writing for Cultural Sensitivity

Techniques:

- **Tone and Formality**: Adapt the level of formality based on cultural norms. For instance, **American** emails may be informal, while **French** emails often maintain a more formal tone.
- **Cultural Sensitivity**: Using culturally appropriate language enhances **ethos** by demonstrating respect and awareness of the audience's values.

Example: An email intended for an **American** audience may start with *"Hi [Name],"* while an email for a **French** audience would use *"Dear Mr./Ms. [Name]"* to convey respect.

Avoiding Idioms and Jargon in Persuasive Cross-Cultural Writing

Importance: Idioms, slang, and culturally specific references can lead to miscommunication.

Best Practice:

- Use **clear, culturally neutral language** to enhance **logos** and make the message accessible to all audiences.

Example: Avoid using phrases like *"**hit the ground running**,"* which may confuse non-native speakers. Instead, use straightforward phrases like *"**start immediately**."*

Best Practices for Persuasive Writing for a Diverse Audience

Crafting Messages:

- **Respect Cultural Differences**: Be mindful of cultural nuances in tone, language, and content.
- **Use Simple Language**: Avoid complex vocabulary or humor that may not translate well.

- **Inclusive Language**: Use **non-discriminatory terms** that respect gender, race, age, and disabilities.

Example: Adapting a proposal for a **Middle Eastern** audience by increasing language formality and avoiding culturally inappropriate humor, ensuring the message respects local values.

Inclusive Language

Non-Discriminatory Style:

- **Gender**: Use gender-neutral terms like *"they/them"* or *"individual"*.
- **Race**: Avoid stereotypes or marginalizing language.
- **Disability**: Use **person-first language**, such as *"person with a disability"* instead of *"disabled person"*.
- **Age**: Refrain from using labels like *"old"* or *"young"*; focus on context or relevant experience instead.

Challenges in Persuading Cross-Cultural Teams

Common Challenges:

- **Language Barriers**: Misinterpretations due to language differences.
- **Varying Motivational Drivers**: Different cultures have different motivators; for instance, **collectivist cultures** value group harmony, while **individualist cultures** value personal achievement.

Example: To persuade a remote team at a multinational like **SAP** to adopt a new project, emphasize **group success** for collectivist team members and **individual growth** for individualist team members.

Persuasive Strategies for Cross-Cultural Team Management

Effective Methods:

- **Building Trust**: Establish relationships through cultural understanding and empathy.
- **Using Social Proof**: Refer to successful collaboration examples that resonate culturally.

Example: **Microsoft** fosters inclusivity in diverse teams by emphasizing shared goals and using social proof—citing successful initiatives that involved culturally diverse groups.

Chapter Seven:

Crafting Impact: Writing for Digital and Social Media Success

In an era where information travels faster than the blink of an eye, the ability to craft compelling, impactful content is no longer a luxury—it's a necessity. Welcome to Chapter Seven, where we embark on a journey into the dynamic realm of digital and social media writing, a landscape that demands innovation, creativity, and strategic insight. Here, every word counts, and each sentence has the potential to resonate, engage, and inspire action among audiences scattered across the globe.

As the lines between traditional media and the digital world continue to blur, understanding how to effectively communicate in this fast-paced environment has never been more crucial. This chapter is designed to equip you with the tools and techniques needed to not only capture attention but also to sustain it in a world overflowing with information. From mastering the art of concise messaging to leveraging the nuances of different platforms, we'll explore how the principles of storytelling can be adapted to fit the unique demands of digital formats.

Join us as we delve into the science of crafting messages that not only inform but also elevate brands, provoke thought, and spark conversations in the ever-evolving landscape of social media. Together, we will uncover strategies that transform ordinary content into extraordinary narratives capable of making a lasting impact. Whether you're a seasoned writer looking to sharpen your skills or a newcomer eager to make your mark, this chapter promises to illuminate the path to writing for success in the digital age.

The Evolution of Digital Communication

The evolution of communication over the decades illustrates a remarkable shift from traditional media to the dynamic digital landscape we experience today. Before the 1990s, print, television, and radio were the primary means of communication, characterized by one-way messaging and limited audience interaction. However, the advent of the Internet and email in the 1990s marked the beginning of a transformative era, as early websites laid the groundwork for more interactive communication. The 2000s brought the emergence of social media platforms like Facebook in 2004 and Twitter in 2006, along with the increasing role of mobile phones, which began to serve as potent communication tools.

In the 2010s and continuing into the present, the rise of mobile-first platforms—such as Instagram and TikTok—and real-time messaging apps like WhatsApp has further revolutionized how we connect and share information. This shift aligns with Media Richness Theory (1986), which posits that digital communication enhances the richness and immediacy of interactions, as evidenced by Facebook's explosive growth from 1 million users in 2004 to over 2.8 billion by 2020, showcasing the profound impact of these technologies on our social interactions.

The Shift to Mobile Communication

The landscape of digital communication has increasingly shifted toward mobile platforms, with over 60% of web traffic now originating from mobile devices (Statista, 2023). This trend has been further amplified by the rise of messaging apps, such as WhatsApp (launched in 2009) and WeChat (launched in 2011), which have become primary communication tools in numerous countries, fundamentally altering how individuals connect and interact.

The nature of mobile communication tends to favor shorter, more direct messaging formats, reflecting users' preferences for quick and efficient exchanges. This phenomenon aligns with the Uses and Gratifications Theory (1974), which suggests that individuals actively seek specific media to meet their diverse needs and desires. In the context of mobile communication, users are driven by their needs for immediacy, interaction, and instant gratification. A clear illustration of this shift can be seen in the explosive growth of WhatsApp, which reached 2 billion users by 2021, underscoring the platform's role in satisfying users' evolving communication preferences in an increasingly mobile-centric world.

Trends In Digital Communication (2020s)

The digital communication landscape has been significantly transformed by the emergence of personalization, ephemeral content, and the dominance of short-form videos. Algorithms now play a central role in shaping user experiences, as seen with platforms like Netflix and YouTube, which tailor content recommendations to individual preferences, enhancing engagement and satisfaction.

Meanwhile, ephemeral content—such as that offered on Snapchat and Instagram Stories—has gained immense popularity due to its fleeting nature, creating a sense of urgency and immediacy among users. Additionally, the rise of platforms like TikTok has driven the short-form video trend, offering a dynamic way for users to create and consume content in bite-sized segments. This rapid evolution can be understood through the lens of Media Dependency Theory (1976), which posits that users increasingly rely on digital platforms for both communication and entertainment.

TikTok's remarkable growth from 200 million users in 2018 to over 1 billion by 2022 exemplifies this trend, as it has become a pivotal platform shaping the landscape of digital content consumption and interaction in an era defined by immediacy and personalization.

Global Usage of Digital Communication

The global usage of digital communication demonstrates a diverse landscape shaped by regional preferences. In Asia, platforms like WeChat and Line dominate the market, providing multifunctional services beyond messaging. In India, WhatsApp is frequently utilized for both personal and business communication, showcasing its versatility. In North America and Europe, Facebook, Instagram, and LinkedIn have established themselves as primary platforms for both professional networking and personal interactions. Meanwhile, Latin America relies heavily on WhatsApp as the main communication tool for a range of interactions, emphasizing its widespread adoption in both personal and business contexts.

This varied usage can be analyzed through Hofstede's Cultural Dimensions Theory (1980), which indicates that communication styles are heavily influenced by cultural dimensions such as individualism and collectivism. A prime example is WeChat in China; with over 1.2 billion monthly users as of 2022, it extends far beyond messaging to include integrated payments, services, and social interactions, reflecting the collectivist values prevalent in Chinese culture.

Cultural Significance of Digital Communication

Understanding the cultural significance of digital communication underscores the differences in communication styles across cultures. In high-context cultures, such as Japan and South Korea, preferences lean towards indirect and subtle forms of communication. This is evident in the popularity of LINE in Japan, which facilitates nuanced interactions. Conversely, low-context cultures, like the USA and Germany, favor direct and explicit communication. In international business, recognizing and adapting to local norms is essential for successful communication.

This cultural dimension can be further explored through Hall's High-Context vs. Low-Context Communication theory (1976). LINE's success in Japan over Facebook exemplifies this theory, as it caters to the country's preference for more private and subtle communication formats.

The Popularity of Social Media Platforms Globally

Globally, the popularity of social media platforms continues to rise. Facebook, founded in 2004, boasts approximately 2.9 billion users worldwide, while YouTube, established in 2005, has 2.5 billion monthly active users. However, regional variations exist, with WeChat dominating in China and VK being popular in Russia. The emergence of platforms like Instagram Reels (introduced in 2020) and TikTok (launched in 2016) highlights a global shift toward short-form video content, reflecting changing user preferences.

Advantages of Digital Communication

Digital communication offers numerous advantages, including the ability to engage in real-time communication that facilitates instant feedback, such as through live chats and social media comments. It also provides businesses with a global reach, allowing them to connect with audiences worldwide at minimal costs. Additionally, digital communication is data-driven, enabling content to be tailored based on analytics and engagement rates. A prime example is Coca-Cola's "*Share a Coke*" campaign (2014), which utilized personalized names on bottles to drive social media engagement and boost global sales.

Writing for Engagement in the Digital Age

Crafting effective content in the digital age hinges on several key strategies. Brevity is essential to capture users' short attention spans, while incorporating interactive elements like polls and quizzes can enhance engagement. Visual appeal, through images and videos, is also crucial for increasing interaction rates. BuzzFeed's quizzes and listicles exemplify these techniques, consistently generating high levels of audience engagement.

Writing for Customer Engagement and Loyalty

To foster customer engagement and loyalty, digital communication must prioritize personalization and consistency. Tailoring emails and messages to reflect individual preferences can significantly enhance user experience. Maintaining a consistent brand voice across various platforms helps build trust and recognition. Amazon's approach to personalized email recommendations based on user activity exemplifies this strategy, effectively driving repeat purchases.

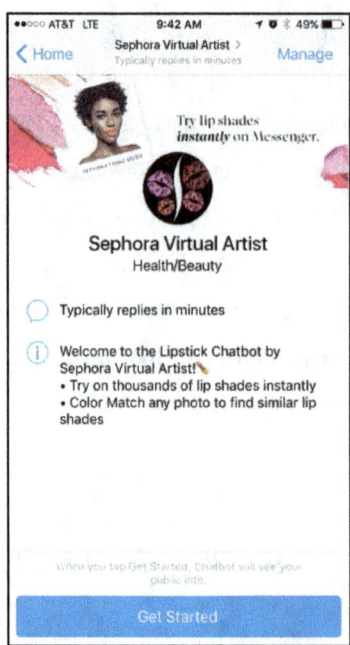

The Role of AI in Digital Communication

Artificial intelligence (AI) is increasingly integral to digital communication, with applications ranging from automating customer service through AI chatbots to generating marketing copy. For instance, Sephora's chatbot, introduced in 2017, assists customers in finding products, enhancing both engagement and sales through instantaneous responses.

Tools for Enhancing Digital Writing

Several tools can enhance digital writing and communication effectiveness. Grammarly ensures clarity and grammatical accuracy, while Canva aids in creating visually appealing digital content. Additionally, Hootsuite automates social media posting and tracking. Research indicates that Grammarly users experience a 76% improvement in clarity and writing consistency, underscoring the tool's value in enhancing communication.

Drawbacks and Precautions in Digital Communication

Despite its advantages, digital communication presents several challenges, including information overload due to constant notifications and content influx. Miscommunication can arise from the lack of non-verbal cues, potentially leading to misunderstandings. Moreover, data privacy risks, such as breaches and the misuse of personal information, necessitate cautious practices. The Cambridge Analytica scandal (2018), where Facebook data was used unethically for political campaigns, highlights the critical need for privacy and ethical considerations in digital communication.

Digital Communication and Privacy

Transparency and data protection are paramount in digital communication. Businesses must clearly inform customers about how their data is collected and used while also implementing robust safeguards against potential breaches. Facebook's data scandal in 2018, wherein Cambridge Analytica used data from 87 million users without consent, prompted tighter privacy regulations and highlighted the urgency of responsible data practices.

Data Security in Digital Communication

To ensure data security in digital communication, implementing encryption for sensitive information and providing employee training on phishing and cybersecurity best practices are essential steps. The 2017 Equifax data breach, which exposed personal information of 147 million individuals, illustrates the imperative for stringent data protection measures.

Social Media Misinformation and Disinformation

The proliferation of misinformation on social media has significant implications for public trust and societal norms. Misinformation has affected various domains, including elections and health issues like COVID-19 vaccine myths. In response, platforms such as Facebook, Twitter, and YouTube have introduced fact-checking mechanisms and content removal policies to combat misinformation. Twitter's measures during the 2020 election to label misleading tweets and ban repeat offenders exemplify proactive efforts to mitigate the spread of false information.

The Rise of Fake News and Deepfakes

Deepfakes represent a troubling trend in digital communication, as AI-generated videos can manipulate reality for entertainment or disinformation purposes. This phenomenon threatens public trust in media and individuals, as demonstrated by a viral deepfake video of Mark Zuckerberg in 2019 that illustrated how easily public figures can be impersonated.

Government Concerns and Regulation of Digital Communication

Government regulations, such as the GDPR (2018) in the EU and the CCPA (2018) in California, are designed to enhance user data protection and transparency. In stark contrast, China maintains strict internet censorship and control through the Great Firewall. Google's €50 million fine in 2019 for failing to provide transparent data consent information highlights the stringent regulatory environment surrounding digital communication.

Ethical Use of Digital Communication

Ethical considerations are critical in digital communication. Businesses must prioritize transparency regarding data use, protect customer privacy, ensure content accuracy, and maintain authenticity in influencer marketing. The Fyre Festival disaster (2017), where influencers promoted the event without awareness of its shortcomings, led to significant backlash and underscores the importance of aligning influencer endorsements with brand values. Conversely, Apple's privacy-focused advertising (2021) demonstrates a proactive approach to user trust by emphasizing its commitment to data protection.

Key Takeaways

- **Follow privacy laws**: Ensure compliance with global data protection regulations.
- **Avoid clickbait**: Use truthful headlines that reflect the content.
- **Respect cultural norms**: Be mindful of cultural differences when crafting global messages.
- **Ethical Communication:** Transparency, accuracy, and cultural sensitivity should be at the core of all digital communication.
- **Respect for Privacy:** Businesses must prioritize data security and adhere to regulations.

Examples:

- Microsoft's inclusivity campaign ensures that marketing content is diverse and respectful of global audiences.
- Apple and Patagonia stand out for their commitment to ethical communication and privacy.

Chapter Eight:

Effective Communication Strategies for Crisis Management

In an increasingly interconnected world, the inevitability of crises poses significant challenges for organizations across all sectors. Whether stemming from natural disasters, technological failures, or reputational mishaps, crises can arise unexpectedly and threaten not only operational continuity but also the trust and loyalty of stakeholders. In these high-pressure situations, the ability to communicate effectively becomes paramount. This chapter dives into the essential communication strategies that organizations must deploy to navigate crises successfully.

Effective crisis communication is not merely a reactive measure; it is a proactive framework that encompasses a range of theories, principles, and practical guidelines. It aims to minimize reputational damage, restore stakeholder confidence, and foster an environment of transparency and understanding. Drawing on established theories such as Situational Crisis Communication Theory and Apologia Theory, this chapter will explore how organizations can categorize crises and tailor their responses accordingly. We will also examine the critical role of language and tone in shaping the perception of messages, highlighting the importance of empathy and clarity in communication.

This chapter further unpacks the principles of effective crisis communication, such as transparency, consistency, and responsiveness, which are vital when addressing customer complaints and engaging with the public. By analyzing real-world case studies, readers will gain insights into the repercussions of poor communication while learning the best practices that can mitigate damage and foster resilience. Ultimately, this guide aims to equip organizations with the tools and knowledge necessary to manage crises effectively, ensuring they emerge not just intact but also stronger, with fortified relationships with their stakeholders.

Theories and Principles of Crisis Communication

Crisis communication is a crucial practice that addresses unexpected events threatening to tarnish an organization's reputation. These crises can stem from various sources, including product failures, public relations mishaps, or even natural disasters. The primary objective of crisis communication is to minimize reputational damage while reassuring stakeholders, including customers, employees, investors, and the community. By employing effective communication strategies, organizations can navigate through turbulent times and emerge with their credibility intact.

Situational Crisis Communication Theory (SCCT)

Developed by Timothy Coombs (2007), the Situational Crisis Communication Theory (SCCT) categorizes crises into three distinct types: victim, accidental, and preventable.

In a victim crisis, the organization is perceived as a victim of external circumstances, such as a natural disaster that impacts operations. Conversely, an accidental crisis occurs when unintentional harm arises from an organization's actions, like equipment failure or a software glitch. Preventable crises, however, involve situations that could have been avoided through better oversight or operational practices, generally stemming from negligence. Understanding these classifications is vital as it helps organizations determine the most appropriate response strategy, allowing them to tailor their message based on the type of crisis they are facing.

Apologia Theory in Crisis Management

Apologia Theory, developed by William L. Benoit (1995), provides a framework for understanding how organizations can issue effective apologies during a crisis. This theory comprises several strategies, including the denial of allegations, efforts to reduce offensiveness by minimizing perceived harm, and corrective action aimed at outlining measures to prevent future occurrences. Apologia strategies often leverage rhetorical techniques, such as narratives and emotional appeals, to persuade the audience and foster understanding.

In conjunction with the Apologia Theory, Image Restoration Theory focuses specifically on strategies to repair an organization's image. This theory highlights techniques like mortification, which involves direct apologies to showcase remorse, and bolstering, where positive aspects of the organization are highlighted to offset the crisis.

Types of Crises

Understanding the different types of crises is fundamental in shaping effective communication strategies on how to address them. Crises can vary in nature and impact, each requiring a tailored approach. Stakeholders must recognize these distinctions to craft messages that resonate effectively with those affected. Additionally, organizations can prepare templates and communication plans for each crisis type, allowing for swift and proactive engagement with their audience when crises arise.

Principles of Crisis Communication

Several key principles underpin effective crisis communication. Transparency is paramount; honest communication builds trust with stakeholders who may be concerned or confused. Consistency across all communication channels ensures that the organization's message remains coherent and clear, reducing the risks of misunderstandings. Responsiveness is equally critical; timely communication can significantly reduce speculation and panic among stakeholders. It is essential to clarify the situation by providing clear, factual information that addresses the concerns of those impacted. Reassuring stakeholders about future safety measures can also help soothe anxieties. Moreover, maintaining trust and goodwill through language that fosters confidence is a vital part of effective crisis communication.

Customer Complaints During Crises

During crises, customer complaints can significantly increase, making it imperative for organizations to have structured strategies for managing these interactions. Several techniques can be employed to navigate through customer complaints effectively. The first step involves active listening, where representatives should concentrate fully on what the customer is conveying. Asking clarifying questions can help gather essential details to understand the issue better. Following this, it is crucial to exhibit empathy and acknowledgment by validating the customer's feelings and providing a sincere apology for any inconvenience caused. Taking responsibility is also important; organizations should own the problem and commit to resolving it, regardless of fault.

A solution-oriented approach should follow, where representatives present options available to customers, allowing them to have some control over the resolution process. Additionally, follow-up is critical to ensure customer satisfaction after resolving the issue. Continuous improvement practices should be documented to gather feedback and identify trends that can inform future enhancements in customer service. Training staff members on effective complaint handling and maintaining a positive attitude throughout all interactions can further improve the customer experience during crises.

Case Study Overview: United Airlines Incident (2017)

A notable case study highlighting the importance of effective crisis communication is the United Airlines incident in 2017, where a passenger was forcibly removed from a flight due to overbooking. Initially, United Airlines responded defensively, lacking empathy towards the passenger and the public's outrage. However, they later issued a more effective apology that acknowledged the incident's impact. This case underscores a critical learning point in crisis management: organizations must acknowledge responsibility for their actions and outline corrective measures to rebuild public trust.

Language and Business Writing Skills

Tone And Language for Crisis Communication

The tone utilized during a crisis communication is essential as it conveys the organization's compassion and respect towards affected parties. For instance, a response that simply states, *"We apologize for the inconvenience,"* lacks the emotional depth necessary during crises. In contrast, saying, *"We understand how upsetting this must be, and we sincerely apologize,"* demonstrates a greater level of empathy and understanding, thereby fostering a stronger connection with stakeholders.

Structuring Apology Statements

Structuring apology statements involves key components that ensure clarity and understanding. An effective apology statement should start by acknowledging the issue, stating, *"We recognize the problem."* Following this, it is essential to express empathy, for example, *"We are deeply sorry for the inconvenience."* The organization should then highlight corrective action, indicating, *"We have taken steps to ensure this doesn't happen again."* Finally, a well-crafted statement can culminate in a reaffirmation of commitment, such as, *"We apologize sincerely and are committed to making it right."*

Clarity and Simplicity in Crisis Messages

Utilizing simple, jargon-free language is vital during crisis communication. By opting for straightforward expressions, organizations can avoid confusion and misinterpretation among stakeholders. For instance, rather than stating, *"We are facing operational contingencies,"* a clearer message would be, *"We are dealing with unexpected issues."* Practicing the rewriting of complex crisis messages into clearer language can significantly enhance understanding.

Positive Language During Crises

Employing positive language during crises can help shift the focus from difficulties to potential solutions. A negative statement like, *"We cannot fulfill your request,"* can be rephrased positively to, *"We're exploring solutions to fulfill your request."* This intentional framing reassures customers and diminishes frustration, demonstrating an organization's commitment to   resolving   issues.

Grammar Tips for Crisis Communication

Clear and effective grammar is crucial in crisis communication. Simple sentence structures should be employed to maintain clarity and avoid confusion. For example, the phrase, *"Due to unforeseen circumstances impacting our production which are beyond our control,"* can be simplified to, *"Due to unforeseen circumstances, production is impacted."* Such revisions enhance readability, ensuring that the message reaches stakeholders effectively.

Word Choice and Empathy

Choosing empathetic words in crisis communication can significantly impact how messages are perceived. Terms like *"understand,"* *"sorry,"* and *"working hard"* convey a sense of empathy and care. For instance, a simple acknowledgement stating, *"We understand your frustration, and we are working hard to resolve the issue,"* can foster a supportive environment during   challenging   times.

Writing Sample: Apology for Data Breach

In the event of a data breach, a well-articulated apology is essential. A sample statement could include, *"We sincerely apologize for the breach that occurred. We understand the impact this has on your trust. We are enhancing our security protocols and are committed to keeping your information safe.*" This statement highlights acknowledgment, empathy, corrective action, and reassurance.

Writing Sample: Product Recall Notice

In the scenario of a product recall, clarity is essential to maintain customer trust. A suitable statement would read, *"We have identified an issue with our product's battery that could impact its safety. We are recalling the affected products to ensure your safety and will provide replacements at no cost."* This statement succinctly addresses the issue, reassuring customers of their safety and the organization's commitment to their well-being.

Common Mistakes in Crisis Communication

Several pitfalls can undermine crisis communication efforts. Organizations often falter by avoiding responsibility, using phrases like, *"If anyone was offended...,"* rather than taking ownership with, *"We apologize for offending our customers."* Additionally, vague commitments such as, *"We are working on it,"* can leave stakeholders feeling uncertain. Clear commitments, such as, *"We have a dedicated team working to fix this issue within the next 48 hours,"* add credibility and instill confidence.

Complaint And Response Letter Examples

Complaint Letter Example

Dear Customer Service Team,

I recently purchased a [Product Name] from your website, and I am disappointed with my experience. The product arrived late and was defective upon unboxing. Despite multiple attempts to reach your support team, I have yet to receive a response.

I am requesting a full refund for the item and an explanation for the delay in handling my inquiries. Please address this issue promptly, as I have been a loyal customer and expected better service.

Sincerely,
[Customer Name]

Response Letter Example With Analysis

Dear [Customer Name],

Thank you for reaching out and sharing your experience with us. We are sorry to hear about the issues you faced and understand how this must have affected your trust in our services.
(Acknowledge the complaint and show empathy.)

We apologize for the delayed delivery and the defective product. After investigating the issue, we found a temporary delay in our shipping department, which affected several orders.
(Take accountability and provide explanation.)

We have processed a full refund for your order and are also providing a 10% discount on your next purchase as a token of our appreciation for your patience and loyalty.
(Resolve the issue and offer a gesture of goodwill.)

We have also updated our customer service processes to ensure faster response times in the future. Should you have any further concerns, please reach out directly to our support team at [Contact   *Information].*

(Assure the customer of future improvements.)

Sincerely,
[Customer Service Manager]

Analysis by Paragraph

1. **Opening:** Acknowledges the complaint and expresses empathy, establishing rapport with the customer.

2. **Apology and Explanation:** Takes accountability for the delay, clarifying the root cause while maintaining transparency.

3. **Resolution and Goodwill Gesture:** Offers a full refund along with a discount, demonstrating commitment to customer satisfaction and goodwill.

4. **Future Assurance:** Promises improvements in response time, providing customers with reassurances about future interactions.

By understanding the intricacies of crisis communication, organizations can navigate crises with greater agility and effectiveness, ultimately preserving their reputation and stakeholder trust during challenging times.

Chapter Nine:

Crisis Management Mastery: Techniques and Writing Skills for Success

As we transition from our exploration of crisis management fundamentals, we delve deeper into the intricate strategies and communication skills essential for mastering crisis resolution. In today's rapidly evolving business landscape, the ability to effectively navigate crises is vital for sustaining customer trust and brand reputation. Whether addressing a dissatisfied customer, responding to an operational failure, or managing a reputational challenge, the techniques outlined in this chapter aim to empower organizations to convert potential setbacks into opportunities for growth.

This chapter builds on foundational concepts in crisis management by introducing critical theories and frameworks that inform effective practices. We will examine the service recovery paradox, which highlights the potential for turning negative experiences into powerful loyalty-building opportunities. Additionally, we will explore Justice Theory in complaint handling, emphasizing the importance of fairness in customer interactions, as well as Expectancy Disconfirmation Theory, which explains the relationship between customer expectations and satisfaction.

Moreover, we will discuss the pivotal role that managers play in fostering a culture of proactive and empathetic crisis management. By equipping their teams with the necessary skills and empowering them to act independently, managers can ensure that complaints are addressed efficiently, reinforcing customer relationships even during challenging times.

As we embark on this journey through advanced crisis management techniques, we aim not only to provide practical tools for resolution but also to illustrate the profound impact that effective communication can have during turbulent moments. Mastering these skills is not just about crisis resolution; it is about transforming crises into stepping stones for lasting customer loyalty and organizational resilience.

Service Recovery Paradox

Service recovery paradox posits that an organization can enhance customer loyalty through exceptional complaint resolution, potentially exceeding the loyalty of customers who have never faced an issue at all. This counterintuitive notion emphasizes the transformative power of turning setbacks into valuable opportunities for relationship building. The service recovery paradox revolves around two key elements: opportunity recognition and resolution quality. Recognizing complaints as opportunities to strengthen relationships is a critical mindset for businesses. It encourages teams to engage positively with customers, rather than dread interactions over dissatisfaction.

Resolution quality is another vital aspect whereby exceeding standard service protocols during the resolution process leaves a lasting positive impression. For example, imagine a hotel guest encountering a booking error who is subsequently upgraded to a suite, treated to a complimentary dinner, and given a personalized, heartfelt apology. This guest may depart more satisfied than if their original booking had been flawless. However, it is crucial to discuss the appropriate levels of compensation and service enhancement for various complaints, as well as the potential limitations of the service recovery paradox, especially in situations of repeated failures.

Justice Theory in Complaint Handling

Justice Theory provides a valuable lens for examining customer satisfaction through the framework of fairness, highlighting three distinct dimensions: distributive justice, procedural justice, and interactional justice.

Distributive justice ensures that customers receive fair outcomes, such as timely refunds or replacements for faulty products. Procedural justice emphasizes the importance of transparent and efficient complaint resolution processes, which enable customers to feel their grievances are handled fairly. Interactional justice focuses on the need for respectful and empathetic treatment during customer interactions, creating a positive experience even amidst dissatisfaction.

For instance, in a scenario where a customer receives a defective product, the principles of justice theory can be applied as follows: distributive justice ensures the customer receives a prompt refund, procedural justice guarantees that the return process is straightforward and easy to navigate, and interactional justice underscores the necessity of treating the customer with empathy and understanding. This framework raises important discussion points, such as which dimension customers prioritize in various contexts and how businesses can design complaint-handling processes that uphold all three aspects of justice.

Expectancy Disconfirmation Theory

Expectancy Disconfirmation Theory posits that customer satisfaction hinges on the gap between expectations and actual service outcomes. This theory introduces the concept of *disconfirmation*, which can manifest in two ways: positive disconfirmation—where outcomes exceed expectations and lead to increased satisfaction—and negative disconfirmation—where outcomes fall short of expectations, resulting in decreased satisfaction. For example, if a customer anticipates an apology for a delayed delivery but instead receives a full refund along with a discount code, the unexpected resolution of their issue may dramatically boost their satisfaction.

However, the application of the theory also raises important questions for businesses. Is it feasible to consistently exceed expectations across all types of complaints? Moreover, organizations must consider how to balance the act of exceeding expectations with the need to maintain profitability, ensuring that customer loyalty does not come at an unsustainable cost.

Managerial Role in Crisis and Complaint Resolution

In the realm of crisis and complaint resolution, the role of management is pivotal. Managers must foster a culture of proactive and empathetic complaint handling, which begins with establishing clear standards for service excellence. Key responsibilities of managers include training teams to equip them with the essential tools and techniques needed for effective complaint resolution, making swift decisions to prevent issues from escalating, and empowering frontline employees to handle minor complaints independently.

For example, consider how Amazon empowers its customer service representatives to issue refunds for low-cost items without requiring managerial approval. This practice streamlines the complaint resolution process and enhances customer satisfaction by enabling swift action that leaves customers feeling valued. By empowering employees, managers can create an environment that prioritizes customer experience and reinforces the organization's commitment to resolving issues effectively, thereby mitigating potential crises before they escalate.

In conclusion, mastering crisis management is an evolving and critical necessity for businesses today. By understanding and implementing key theories and frameworks such as the service recovery paradox, Justice Theory, Expectancy Disconfirmation Theory, and recognizing the managerial role in complaint resolution, organizations can navigate crises with agility, transforming challenges into opportunities for growth and customer loyalty.

Stages of Effective Complaint Handling

1. **Acknowledgment:**
   Recognizing the issue and expressing empathy sets a positive tone and reassures customers that their concerns are taken seriously.
   o **Sample Phrasing:** *"Thank you for bringing this to our attention. We sincerely apologize for the inconvenience."*

2. **Resolution:**
   Offering solutions that are proportional to the complaint ensures fairness and satisfaction.
   o **Strategies:** Provide clear options such as refunds, replacements, or discounts.
   o **Sample Phrasing:** *"We've processed a full refund and would like to offer a 10% discount on your next purchase."*

3. **Follow-Up:**
   Ensuring the resolution meets the customer's expectations reinforces their trust.
   o **Sample Phrasing:** *"Please let us know if there's anything more we can do to ensure your satisfaction."*

Advanced Language and Tone for Complaint Handling

Using the right language and tone can de-escalate tensions and foster positive outcomes.

Empathy vs. Defensiveness:

- **Empathetic Language:** *"We understand how frustrating this must have been for you."*
- **Defensive Language to Avoid:** *"It's not our fault this happened."*

Language Adjustment Table:

Problematic Phrasing	Improved Phrasing
"We can't help you with this issue."	*"Let me see how we can resolve this for you."*
"That's company policy."	*"Here's what we can do to assist you."*

Memo Writing for Internal Investigations

Internal investigation memos serve as a crucial tool for documenting complaints, facilitating investigations, and guiding improvements within the company. Unlike formal reports or communications that might be addressed to external stakeholders, internal memos provide a more immediate and accessible means of communication among employees and departments. Their significance cannot be overstated, particularly during internal investigations, where clarity, transparency, and accountability are paramount.

Internal memos play an instrumental role in meticulously documenting complaints and concerns raised by employees. By establishing a formal record, organizations create a framework that allows for a thorough and systematic approach to addressing issues. This documentation is invaluable during an investigation, as it serves as a point of reference for all involved parties. It ensures that complaints are not swept under the rug or forgotten, but rather are given the attention they deserve within the organizational framework. When drafting memos, it is imperative to provide a clear description of the issue, including relevant details such as dates, individuals involved, and the specific nature of the complaint. This precision is essential for guiding subsequent investigations and for ensuring a comprehensive understanding of the matter at hand.

A well-structured internal memo does more than merely document a complaint; it strengthens transparency and facilitates informed decision-making. By promoting a culture of open communication, memos allow team members to share concerns without fear of repercussions, fostering a safe environment where issues can be addressed constructively. When managers and employees are informed about the complaints and ongoing investigations, they are better equipped to understand the organizational context and can contribute to discussions about potential solutions.

Additionally, a well-crafted memo provides a roadmap for decision-making. It sets out the context and background information, allowing leadership to evaluate the situation with clarity. In essence, it transforms potentially convoluted information into a streamlined narrative that aids in identifying the appropriate course of action to address the complaint. By illuminating the steps taken in response to the complaint, internal memos contribute to a holistic understanding of the situation, empowering those in leadership positions to make sound, evidence-based decisions.

Structure:

1. **Header Information:** Include recipient, sender, date, and subject.
2. **Introduction:** State the purpose and provide context for the investigation.
3. **Investigation Findings:** Use bullet points for clarity.
4. **Root Cause Analysis:** Identify the underlying issues.
5. **Proposed Solutions:** Outline actionable recommendations.
6. **Conclusion:** Summarize findings and next steps.

Sample Memo Excerpt:

To: [Management]
From: [Your Name]
Date: [Date]
Subject: ***Investigation Summary: Order Delay Issue***

Introduction:

This memo summarizes the investigation into a delayed shipment complaint.

Findings:

- The shipment was delayed by five days due to staffing shortages.
- Communication protocols were inconsistently followed.

Proposed Actions:

- Implement contingency staffing plans for peak seasons.
- Update customer service protocols to ensure consistent follow-up communication.

Key Takeaways

- Effective crisis management transforms challenges into opportunities to strengthen customer relationships.
- Applying frameworks like the Service Recovery Paradox and Justice Theory ensures consistent and empathetic complaint handling.
- Advanced language techniques and structured memos contribute to resolving issues professionally and efficiently.

By mastering these skills, businesses can navigate crises with confidence, ultimately enhancing customer trust and loyalty.

Chapter Ten:

Persuasive Presentations: Strategies for Meaningful Communication

The ability to convey ideas persuasively is a transformative skill that can turn routine presentations into powerful catalysts for change. As leaders, colleagues, and innovators, we often face the challenge of not just sharing information, but inspiring others to take action and embrace new perspectives. Chapter 10 explores the art and science of persuasive presentations, offering strategies that elevate your message from ordinary to extraordinary.

At the core of effective communication is a deep understanding of your audience—a diverse mix of emotions, motivations, and viewpoints. This chapter will guide you in crafting messages that resonate, employing storytelling techniques, emotional appeals, and logical arguments to create presentations that capture attention and foster connection. We will emphasize the importance of authenticity in persuasion, underscoring that genuine influence must be built on honesty and ethical considerations.

Prepare to discover how to structure your presentation for maximum impact, the power of visuals to enhance your narrative, and practical techniques for engaging your audience in meaningful dialogue. Mastering these strategies will equip you to inform, inspire, and motivate in ways that leave a lasting impression.

As we explore persuasive presentations, remember that you have the ability to shape perceptions, ignite passion, and drive change. Let's uncover the tools and insights that will empower you to communicate with purpose and influence, making your message not just heard, but truly felt.

Importance of Persuasion

Influence decision-making:

Persuasive presentations can sway opinions and encourage specific actions.

Example: A sales pitch that convinces potential customers to purchase a product.

Inspire action:

Effective persuasion can motivate people to take action, such as volunteering or donating.

Example: A non-profit organization's presentation that inspires donations.

Build credibility and trust:

Establishing yourself as a credible and trustworthy speaker enhances your persuasive power.

Example: A keynote speech that establishes the speaker's authority on a subject.

From Mediocre to Masterful

Transitioning from a mediocre communicator to a masterful one is an empowering journey that involves both self-awareness and deliberate practice. It requires a commitment to refining your skills, embracing feedback, and cultivating an authentic voice that resonates with your audience. Below, we explore the qualities that define this transformation, offering insights into how to elevate your communication from the ordinary to the extraordinary.

Key Elements and Qualities

Clarity

The presentation should be clear and easy to understand. This includes clear speech, well-organized content, and straightforward visuals.

Engagement

The ability to capture and maintain the audience's attention. This can be achieved through storytelling, interactive elements, and dynamic delivery.

Confidence

The presenter should appear confident and knowledgeable about the topic. This helps to establish credibility and trust with the audience.

Relevance

The content should be relevant to the audience's interests and needs. Tailoring the presentation to the audience can make it more impactful.

Visual aids

Effective use of visual aids such as slides, videos, and charts can enhance understanding and retention of the information.

Structure

A well-structured presentation with a clear beginning, middle, and end helps the audience follow along and understand the key points.

Conciseness

Being concise and to the point helps to keep the audience's attention and ensures that the main messages are communicated effectively.

Passion

Showing enthusiasm and passion for the topic can be contagious and make the presentation more compelling.

Preparation

Thorough preparation and practice can help ensure a smooth delivery and the ability to handle questions or unexpected issues.

Audience interaction

Engaging with the audience through questions, discussions, or activities can make the presentation more interactive and memorable.

Storytelling

Using stories or anecdotes to illustrate points can make the presentation more relatable and engaging.

Body language

Effective use of body language, including eye contact, gestures, and movement, can enhance communication and engagement.

Preparing Your Presentation

The process of preparing a presentation is a critical stage that sets the foundation for its success. How you approach this phase can mean the difference between a mediocre delivery and a masterful performance. In this section, we will explore the qualities that distinguish average preparatory practices from exceptional ones and provide strategies for elevating your presentation preparation to a higher standard.

I. Understanding Your Audience

- **Demographics (age, gender, education):** Tailor your message to the demographic characteristics of your audience.
- **Psychographics (interests, values, attitudes):** Understand what motivates your audience and their values.

- **Needs and expectations**: Address the specific needs and expectations of your audience.

Example: Analyzing an audience of potential investors vs. Employees.

II. Setting Clear Objectives

Define **SMART** objectives for a sample presentation.

Key Points:

- *Specific*: Clearly define what you want to achieve.
- *Measurable*: Ensure your objectives can be measured.
- *Achievable*: Set realistic goals.
- *Relevant*: Align your objectives with your overall goals.
- *Time-bound*: Set a timeframe for achieving your objectives.

III. Building a Strong Argument

- Engaging audience's *emotions*
- Making your message *memorable*
- To keep your audience *engaged* throughout.

Logical reasoning (logos):

Use facts and logical arguments to support your message.

Emotional appeal (pathos):

Connect with your audience on an emotional level.

Credibility (ethos):

Establish your credibility and authority on the subject.

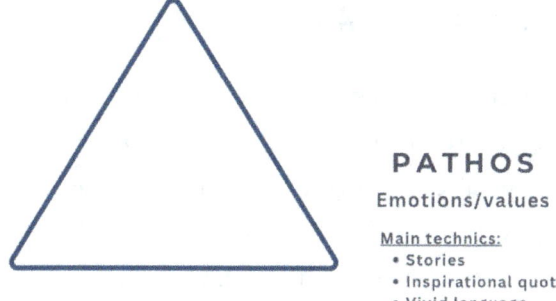

LOGOS

Logic/reason/proof

Main technics:
- Structure of the speech (opening/body/conclusion)
- References to studies, statistics, case studies...
- Comparisons, analogies, and metaphors

ETHOS

Credibility/trust

Main technics:
- Personal branding
- Confidence in delivery
- Cites credible sources

PATHOS

Emotions/values

Main technics:
- Stories
- Inspirational quotes
- Vivid language

IV. Crafting a Compelling Message

Overview:

- **Introduction (hook, attention seeking techniques):** Capture attention with a strong opening and clearly state your main idea.
- **Body (main points, supporting evidence):** Organize your main points logically and support them with evidence.
- **Conclusion (summary, call to action):** Summarize your main points and encourage your audience to take action.

V. Overcoming Nervousness

- **Preparation and practice:** Thoroughly prepare and practice your presentation to build confidence.
- **Relaxation techniques:** Use deep breathing, visualization, and other relaxation techniques to calm nerves.
- **Positive visualization:** Visualize a successful presentation to boost confidence.

Taking the Spotlight

The pivotal moment of stepping onto the stage is often accompanied by a mix of excitement and anxiety. To make the most of this opportunity, it's essential to embrace confidence, maintain positive body language, and engage the audience with an attention-grabbing opening. Making eye contact fosters a connection, while pacing and controlled breathing help articulate thoughts clearly. Embracing the reality of mistakes as learning opportunities can also ease performance nerves. Ultimately, focusing on delivering the message rather than the fear of speaking allows presenters to transform their first moments in the spotlight into impactful experiences for both themselves and their audience.

Creating a Strong Opening

- **Capturing *attention***: Use a hook to grab the audience's attention from the start.
- **Establishing *relevance***: Explain why the topic is important to the audience.
- **Setting the *tone***: Set the tone for the rest of the presentation.

Engaging Your Audience

Key points:

- **Asking questions**: Engage your audience by asking questions and encouraging participation.
- **Interactive elements**: Use polls, quizzes, or other interactive elements to keep your audience engaged.
- **Handling distractions**: Stay focused and address distractions calmly and professionally.

Using Evidence and Examples

- **Types of evidence (statistics, testimonials, case studies):** Use various types of evidence to support your arguments.
- **Relevance and reliability:** Ensure your evidence is relevant and from reliable sources.
- **How to integrate evidence effectively:** Seamlessly incorporate evidence into your presentation.

Developing Your Delivery Style

- **Confidence and enthusiasm:** Speak confidently and with enthusiasm to engage your audience.
- **Body language and gestures:** Use open, positive body language and purposeful gestures to emphasize points.
- **Eye contact:** Maintain eye contact to connect with your audience.

Visual Aids

Visual aids are powerful tools that enhance presentations by making complex information more accessible and engaging. They can include slides, charts, graphs, images, videos, and even handouts, all designed to support and illustrate key points. Effective visual aids do not overwhelm the audience; instead, they complement the spoken message, reinforcing important concepts and facilitating understanding. A well-designed visual can capture attention, evoke emotions, and help the audience retain information long after the presentation is over. When used thoughtfully, visual aids transform an ordinary presentation into a dynamic experience, enabling better communication and fostering a deeper connection with the audience.

Developing Your Visual Aids

Visibility

- Readable and consistent font

Clarity

- Make the points easy to understand.
- Avoid busy backgrounds and distracting color combinations

Simplicity

- Avoid busy graphics or distracting clip art

Relevance

- Must be meaningful for the audience

Dos and Don'ts:

Slide 1

- Avoid long paragraphs. It's a slide, not a document.
- Use lots of titles, headings, and bullet points.
- *"No audience ever complained about a presentation being too short."* – Stephen Keague

Slide 2

- Avoid all caps.
- Font sizes are too big.
- Spacing between words is needed.
- Plan your content layout. Don't be afraid of using lots of white space in your slides.
- Use a pre-made PowerPoint or Keynote template.

Slide 3

- It looks dull.
- **Images** should help engage your audience, particularly on this topic.
- Rethink the number of words needed for illustrating your point(s).

Slide 4

- Images and graphics chosen do not help showcase the data without confusing the audience.
- Keep graphic designs easier to understand for all audience.
- Rethink the amount of information needed for illustrating your point(s).

Slide 5

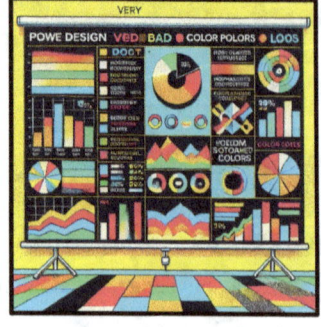

- Using colors that don't highlight the texts. Now the text is unreadable.
- Think twice before using images as the background.
- Prepare a **color palette** that include primary and secondary colors. Stick to them throughout the slides to make them consistent.

Slide 6

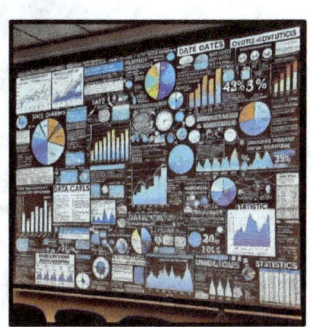

- Stats and data are important but don't include too much into every slide
- Audience won't be able to read it without binoculars.
- Visualize your stats and data. Use **infographics** and **illustrations**.

Handling Objections

- **Listening actively**: Listen carefully to understand the objection.
- **Validating concerns**: Acknowledge and validate the concerns of your audience.
- **Providing clear and concise responses**: Respond clearly and concisely, addressing the concern directly.

Crafting a Memorable Conclusion

- **Summarizing key points**: Recap the main points of your presentation.
- **Call to action**: Encourage your audience to take a specific action.
- **Leaving a lasting impression**: End with a memorable statement or question.

Managing Q&A Sessions

- **Anticipating questions**: Prepare for potential questions and practice your responses.
- **Responding effectively**: Listen carefully, answer clearly and concisely, and stay calm.
- **Staying calm under pressure**: Use relaxation techniques to manage stress during Q&A sessions.

Practice and Feedback

- **Rehearsal techniques**: Practice your presentation multiple times to build confidence and refine your delivery.
- **Seeking constructive feedback**: Get feedback from peers or mentors to identify areas for improvement.
- **Iterative improvement**: Use feedback to make continuous improvements to your presentation.

Common Problems

- Unnatural speech
- Reading directly from a script
- Not enough eye contact
- Speaking too fast or too slowly
- Speaking unclearly
- Boring contents
- Voice too soft
- Ideas not well-organized

How About Some "Quick Fixes"

- **Streamlining Slides**: Limit the amount of information on each slide to avoid overwhelming your audience.
- **Engaging your Audience**: Connect with your audience by speaking naturally rather than reading directly from your slides.
- **Establishing Eye Contact**: Maintain eye contact and actively respond to feedback from your audience.

Effective Use of Voice

The human voice is a vital and beautiful instrument in delivering a compelling presentation, as it conveys not just the content but also the presenter's passion and confidence. Effective use of voice involves several key elements, including tone, volume, pitch, and pacing. A varied tone helps to express emotions and emphasizes important points, while appropriate volume ensures that the audience can hear the message clearly without straining. Pitch variation keeps the audience engaged, preventing monotony, and strategic pacing allows for moments of emphasis and reflection. Pausing at key moments gives the audience time to absorb information and adds drama to the delivery. By mastering these vocal techniques, presenters can captivate their audience, convey authenticity, and leave a lasting impact.

- **Tone and pitch**: Use a variety of tones and pitches to keep your audience engaged.
- **Pace and pausing**: Vary your speaking pace and use pauses for emphasis.
- **Volume and clarity**: Speak clearly and at an appropriate volume for the room.

References

Aristotle. (1926). *Rhetoric* (J. H. Freese, Trans.). Harvard University Press. (Original work published ca. 367–322 BCE)

Ball-Rokeach, S. J., & DeFleur, M. L. (1976). A Dependency Model of Mass Media Effects. *Communication Research, 3*(1), 3–21.

Berlo, D. K. (1960). *The Process of Communication: An Introduction to Theory and Practice.* Holt, Rinehart, and Winston.

Cialdini, R. B. (1984). *Influence: The Psychology of Persuasion*. New York: Harper Business.

Coombs, W. T. (2007). *Protecting organization reputations during a crisis: The development and application of situational crisis communication theory. Corporate Reputation Review, 10*(3), 163-176.

Daft, R. L., & Lengel, R. H. (1986). Organizational Information Requirements, Media Richness, and Structural Design. *Management Science*, 32(5), 554–571.

Hall, E. T. (1976). *Beyond culture*. Doubleday.

Hofstede, G. (1980). *Culture's consequences: International differences in work-related values*. Beverly Hills, CA: Sage.

House, R. J., Hanges, P. J., Javidan, M., Dorfman, P. W., & Gupta, V. (2004). *Culture, Leadership, and Organizations: The GLOBE Study of 62 Societies*. Sage Publications.

Katz, E., Blumler, J. G., & Gurevitch, M. (1974). Uses and gratifications research: The past and the present. *Public Opinion Quarterly*, 36(1), 509-523. https://doi.org/10.1086/268201

Lewis, R. D. (1996). *When Cultures Collide: Leading Across Cultures*. Nicholas Brealey Publishing.

Monroe, A. H. (1943). *Principles of Speech*. Scott, Foresman, and Company.

Pexels. (n.d.). *Pexels homepage*. Retrieved December 19, 2024, from https://www.pexels.com

Schramm, W. (1954). *The Process and Effects of Mass Communication*. University of Illinois Press.

Shannon, C. E., & Weaver, W. (1949). *The Mathematical Theory of Communication*. University of Illinois Press.

Statista. (2023). Share of global website traffic from mobile devices 2015–2023. *Statista*. Retrieved December 3, 2024, from https://www.statista.com/statistics/277125/

Trompenaars, F., & Hampden-Turner, C. (1997). *Riding the Waves of Culture: Understanding Diversity in Global Business* (2nd ed.). McGraw-Hill.

Author: Joseph W.C. Lau

Editor: Analisa Sande

Special thanks to Grandiose World Education Foundation (Hong Kong)

GRANDIOSE WORLD

www.ingramcontent.com/pod-product-compliance
Lightning Source LLC
Chambersburg PA
CBHW071519220526
45472CB00003B/1083